ADVICE I IGNORED

Stories and Wisdom from a Formerly Depressed Teen

RUBY WALKER

To you, with all the sharp edges
who needs kindness the most.

CONTENTS

Introduction

If it's hard to get out of bed, this book is for you.
If you're always crying,
Or if the numbness is so cold you beg for something to cry
about, this book is for you.
If you avoid looking in the mirror, even when you're brushing
your teeth, this book is for you.
If you're terrified of the good days because you know they never
last, this book is for you.
If you snap when people ask, "How are you?"
Or if it's hard to speak at all,
I wrote this book for you.

If your kid,
(Your friend,
Your parent,
Sibling,
Spouse)
Is like me, I wrote this book for you, too.

Because selfishly, this book is for me. I wrote it for my 15 year old self, the emo girl who wore all black and cried in class every day until she had to drop out; the girl who was so miserable she couldn't imagine growing up and being an adult; the girl who hated getting advice she knew she wouldn't take. I wrote this book to convince her of the world's biggest cliché—

It gets better.

Advice I Ignored is a catalogue of everything I had to learn about myself so I could finally feel okay. Each chapter is broken into three parts, as I think the process of taking advice is:

1. Hearing good advice. (An essay.)
2. Convincing yourself it's important. (A personal story.)
3. Actually taking it. (Step-by-step instructions.)

Recovery isn't simple or easy, and unlike this book, it doesn't happen in a clear sequence of separate stories. In reality, all of these things were happening in my life at around the same time. They overlapped and affected each other. At the time I had no idea what "lessons" I was supposed to be learning—

I was just trying to survive. But for the sake of clarity, I pulled my story apart into distinct threads.
I hope my 20/20 hindsight is helpful to someone. I hope this book makes you feel less alone.

Content warnings: Chapter two's story, "The More Unsustained," includes a brief discussion of suicide. Chapter five's story, "How We Deal With It," includes memories of sexual trauma. The flashbacks are italicized, and the story can be read without them. The story also includes non-graphic self-harm.

CHAPTER 1

You can do it!

You could do anything if you really wanted to do it. That is to say, anything you have the physical capabilities of doing. You could yell at your Physics teacher. You could start calling your father "Daddy-O." You could go outside completely naked. You could start belting Big Green Tractor in the beer aisle of your local convenience store. You could soak yourself down in the rain of a thunderstorm and try to taste lightning on the water when it drips into your mouth— the skeletons of Earth's first life, aged 3.6 billion years, slipping through your unflossed teeth. Am I getting sidetracked?

You could hurt yourself.
(I hurt myself.)
Or you could stop.
(I stopped.)

So why do the statistics look so dismal? Sometimes it feels like nobody ever really changes. Cheaters are gonna cheat, drinkers are gonna drink. You look around and you can feel it on other people, in yourself: the black morass of powerlessness.

When I'm lying in bed procrastinating, and I know I'm procrastinating, but I'm not going to stop, even though I want to — The Goop. When I can't seem to make myself take a shower — The Goop. When I'm reaching for a drink, and I can already see how this night will end— The Goop. When I'm sad, listening to sad songs just to make myself sadder — The Goop.

The Goop is my term for the notion that my bad behavior is an act of some divinity outside my control. I mean, rationally it doesn't make any sense. If I can scratch my nose, I can clean my room. All I need to do is will my limbs to go to the right places.

So why, then, is it so easy to fall into the Goop? For me it was two sorts of fear. The first was a fear that I really *could* do anything. With endless choices available at every second, what if I made the wrong choice? I'd rather do nothing at all. (Well, doing nothing is a choice, too. I wasn't truly protecting myself by remaining idle.)

And the second was a fear that everything was my fault. After all, if I could have done my homework all along, wasn't I just lazy? If I could recover from depression— does that mean it was my fault in the first place? If I had the power to recover from trauma, to stop caring so much, was it ever really "That Bad"? If I accept that I can change something, if I understand that I've always had power over that thing, the fact that I hadn't changed before reflects badly on me.

I felt like I would collapse under the weight of that guilt. It terrified me. It made me lash out at the mere suggestion that I could control my behavior.

Don't we all know that person? That crowd?

And it's strange to be in this position, because I know for a fact that the person I was would've been so pissed off by the person I am now. I know what it feels like when someone tells you to change. It doesn't feel like an affirming, friendly tip.

It feels like they're saying, "You should just get over this."

"You're making yourself miserable."

"It's all your fault."

That central aversion to being blamed is why I ignored all the good advice I'd ever been given. The changes only started happening when I shifted my perspective.

I'll tell you what I wish I'd known at thirteen:
You don't need to fear free will.
Depression is like any other illness.
There is a genetic factor.
There is an environmental factor.
There is a physiological factor.
And there is you.

Your environment and biology have combined in a perfect storm to afflict you with this mental illness. It isn't your fault you are depressed, but the way that you deal with this illness is in your power. There are things you can do that will make it better, and things you can do that will make it worse. There are ways of thinking that will make it better, and ways of thinking that will make it worse. And just as there is no limit to how bad it can get, there's no limit to how good it can get, either.

STORYTIME: I AM NOT FREE.

Ms. Renteria was saying something to us. Her voice was just a noise to me, like a creaking chair or the scratching sound my Bic pen was making where it had already worn through the paper to grit against my desk. Roll, roll, roll. Metal on enamel, circles on circles, peace.

"Oh." I unclenched my hand, blinking.

There were new things on my desk.

Two maps. A compare/contrast essay between Rome and Han China. Notes on a video. Despite a general unease, I could handle this level of coursework. All year I had managed to scrape up an A. I did all the work during my lunch period some days, sure, but it felt manageable. Or doable. And even when it didn't, I did it anyway. Now something terrible strung hooks into my lungs and pulled hard. I didn't think. I stared at this pile of responsibilities and all at once it all felt like too much. How am I going to do this? Why can't I do this? Please, just stop thinking, I hate this, I'm useless.

The look on my face must have spelled some version of animal terror, or else I looked like I might weep. The blonde girl sitting next to me noticed my extended dramatic staring and turned to me. She asked a simple, genuine question. "Why don't you just do it?"

Anything at all could have ruined that moment. Maybe if I'd had three fewer assignments. Or the girl spoke five minutes later. Or if I'd had just a slightly easier time making myself get dressed that morning. Sydney's good-natured question hurt me so badly because it was a question I'd asked a hundred thousand times with no good answer. I felt the crack of my palm hitting a desk.

The volume of my voice made Sydney flinch back. The class gaped at me. Being angry wasn't helping anymore, not since my chair was attached to my desk and standing up abruptly put me off balance. One of the boys murmured, "Damn," and I fell back into my seat to drown in shame.

Maybe the class was glad I finally broke. I always aced tests without studying. I was cocky. I deserved a downfall. I was that weird kid who talked too much, a walking encyclopedia. I deserved a reason to finally shut up.

Tears and snot stuck to my forearms. Mrs. Renteria was still in the room after everyone else filed out for sixth period. She'd have to deal with my sniffling until I could bottle it up enough to finally leave. I'd be late to chemistry for sure. I kept my head down in the halls.

Hours later, I was staring at the ceiling again. Mom stepped around the mess in my doorway. The hardwood floor creaked softly under the weight of her disappointment. I tried to look up and at 'em, but it wasn't working out. "Ruby," she said, "I told you not to sit in the dark, it's bad for your eyes."

I was quiet for a second. "The sun set. I just…"

She flicked on the glaring overhead light. I reached beside me for my lamp— and, finding the knob at its base, doubled the strain on my maladjusted eyes. "Turn that one off," I said, "It's too bright." She complied.

Mom shifted onto her left foot. "Is your homework done?"

"Yes."

"You're telling the truth?"

"Yes…" I lied.

I couldn't think about the fact that I had school tomorrow. The natural consequence of time's passage seemed like a machine full of gnawing, snaggletoothed gears: Friday promised the same thing I'd survived a hundred times, but it still filled me with visceral terror. Somehow, more of the same was not comforting.

Hays High School was an ugly linoleum panopticon with a Texas-style football fetish. Everyone always expected me to do things. I felt them looking at me. Wondering what went wrong. Making guesses. Passing judgment. Losing patience. Feeling sorry.

Of course, I was not thinking of any of those things. I listened to my faucet drip, and I stared at my ceiling. The faucet was starting to bug me. Drip drip drip. I had a chemistry test tomorrow. Drip drip. I picked at a bump on my forehead. Grease glimmered on my fingertips when I pulled them away. I hadn't showered since — when? Drip drip. I still had an essay to write. Drip.

Alright, let's move. Could I even manage? I tilted my head and fixed my stare on my left arm. Every hair was golden-white in the lamplight. It was still too bright. I would've felt better if Mom had just left me alone.

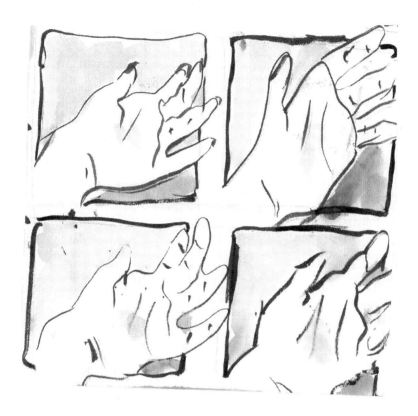

I traced my eyes across the planes of my hand. I imagined closing it into a fist. Nothing. I knew what it felt like to move—why wasn't it happening?

Maybe my arm would move. Maybe I'd stand and shut the faucet off. My hand did not clench— my arm did not move. I would rather lie there wondering, *"Can I move? Will my hand move?"* than think of every ignored responsibility, in a stack towering towards the heavens. It would be easier to do nothing at all. The faucet kept dripping.

I faked sick a few days every week. I knew my mother no longer believed me when I coughed and groaned, but she let me stay home, quietly panicking as her daughter spoke less and less. We discussed homeschooling, and I tried not to show my relief.

"I really don't have to go back? Just like that?"

"Well," she said, "You should go on Monday. Just say goodbye while we wait on the paperwork to go in, okay?"

So I went. February 4th, just a few days shy of my 15th birthday. A winter storm slicked the concrete. My hands stayed in my pockets all day, wary of the cold. I skipped most of my classes, and only mentioned that it was my last day to the five people I thought would care. After almost two years doing acting and tech, my parting gift to Hays' theater department was an art class portfolio, unfinished and abandoned on the dressing room floor.

In those first days after I dropped out, it was nothing but a relief. Every minute of every day in school I'd been micromanaged and pushed around. Failing to meet expectations day in, day out was exhausting. Then, suddenly, nobody expected anything of me. I could wake up wrapped in yesterday's clothes at two in the afternoon, eat three bowls of cereal, and fall back into the half-sleep daze of constant internet use.

After years of "too much, all the time", "nothing at all, ever" was a precious gift.

One morning I woke up frozen in both senses of the word: my toes icy, my mind trapped in stagnation borne from an utter lack of energy.

I went outside and knelt down on the back deck, knees groaning. The air blew cool through my clothes— makeshift now, a shirt with the sleeves ripped off and some leggings cut short. I didn't have to look presentable. Nobody from school had seen me for a month. My friends talked about me like I was dead.

"We miss Ruby," they said. *I'm right here. Come see me, I'm all alone,* my ego didn't let me reply. I pressed my face and the front of my body to the sun-warmed boards.

I needed time to be in the sunshine. It made me feel farther from school than I'd ever been. I could spend all my time outside, if I wanted to. Something about that frightened and excited me. I had so many decisions to make, and even refusing to face them was a decision in itself.

What would I do with my time until camp this summer? How would I manage homeschooling? How would I get into university? Did I want to go to community college? Did I want to get a job? Should I start getting out of bed in the morning? What should I do after that?

I felt the sun start to sting my shoulders and turn my hair red-hot, but I didn't move. There was too much to think about. There was too much to do. Couldn't I just stay there and melt?

I lay on my side, hands in front of me in a gold splotch of sun. It caught against the translucent little hairs on the backs of my knuckles and made them shine white. My fingers didn't move. I knew I had to get up. I hadn't eaten much in the previous few days; I was hollow and hungry.

Can't I do one thing deliberately?

I never considered myself beautiful. Maybe that's why I suddenly loved my hands—and that was it, I loved them! I watched the frozen curves of each one, the wrinkles and planes. I loved them not like well-worn tools, but like art in a museum. They were gorgeous because they weren't mine.

Enough poetic hogwash. I know they're my hands. I just have to move. I just have to get up and do something. Literally anything. The inside of my skin bubbled up, a shaken coke can.

I creaked to life and sat up straight, putting my legs beneath me before the courage could drain out.

Finally.

I stepped deliberately. I found food to eat, an apple and some bread.

If I can get up, surely I can do some dishes. But my motivation went flat as quickly as it had flared. I went back to sleep.

Time passed. I noticed my freedom in those little flickers; sniffles in a dead-silent room. I tested its boundaries one by one. I forced myself to exercise when I was agitated by the sound of human breath, to keep working when I wanted to play around, to be kinder, to hold on, to get a little better. If my hands could move, I could write. If my lungs would open, I could run. It was all just proof. Over and over, proving in tiny increments that I could choose the way I lived.

I was just finishing a run. Not a very long one—it had been a while since I'd gone for any significant distance and I wanted to get home non-sweaty. Lacking headphones, I also had the soundtrack of my labored, asthmatic breathing to enjoy. It was too beautiful outside for music, anyway. My mind just felt crowded when I tried playing some aloud.

I chased the tail end of an early summer rain. Every step I took in the dewy grass shook moisture free, leaving visible footprints. One end of the sky, facing my left was storm. It was purple gray and looming — though I saw no lightning while I looked, it had the appearance of a thunderhead thick and pregnant with static electricity. The other end of the sky was covered in sheets of cursive clouds folding into a magnificent show. Fluffy white clouds sprayed in an arc over the setting sun, so everything was incandescent, even as rain hit my shoulder. But under all of this, I splashed through the puddles on the road, mirrors showing the two-faced sky.

I encountered a verdant field. Soft grass. Rain lilies grew there beside bunches of clover showing shy violet flowers. The left of the field offered yellow daisy blooms, while the right was walled in by a shrub. Even that shrub was turning new, pale green leaves for spring.

I did it because I wanted to and because nothing could stop me. I got on the ground and soaked myself, rolling back-and-forth among flowers. I picked a lily, petted a clover, smelled the sweet grass and tucked a white daisy behind my ear.

I lay on my back and watch the clouds draft a minute. On my way to leave, I hugged that shrub. With my face wet I strode home.

I didn't even regret it when the grass started to make me itch. I reveled in the simple joy of doing exactly what I wanted for no practical reason at all.

There wasn't any deeper secret or revelation. There was no code to break, nor any epiphanies to receive, aside from this: I could. I always could. The power I both pined for and feared was part of me from the very start.

> "You say: I am not free. But I have raised and lowered my arm. Everyone understands that this illogical answer is an irrefutable proof of freedom."
> — Leo Tolstoy, *War and Peace*

ADVICE ON HOW TO GAIN A SENSE OF FREE WILL, VANQUISH THE GOOP, AND FINALLY START TAKING SHOWERS AGAIN:

Tip #1. Start small.

You can't just suddenly decide to not be depressed anymore. That ain't how it works, unfortunately. If you struggle with hygiene like I did, it's very unlikely that you'll wake up one morning spontaneously eager to hop in the shower and scrub.

But the good news is, you don't need to start out all gung-ho and ready to go! You can purposefully build confidence in your ability to do difficult things. You just need to give yourself a real reason to feel that confidence.

So try this: if you're in a slump, sitting around and feeling useless, decide on something small to do. What that something is depends on how bad you feel.

Just pick one little thing and get it done! Even if it's just sitting up in bed. This is proof that you can follow through. Even when you feel absolutely awful, there is something you can do. All these little victories are proof of your power. "*If I can make a bed, I can brush my teeth.*" "*If I can brush my teeth, I can take a shower, I can get dressed—*" And so on. Big accomplishments are just a hundred tiny ones, one after another. You're getting there!

Tip #2. Make a list of "safe" activities. Things you like doing, that don't feel daunting to start.

Now, list some things you want or need to do, but you're unsure about— goals or jobs. Take each of your unsure activities and make it "doable." Instead of thinking, "I can't clean my room, I always get distracted," you can think, "I made my bed today, so there's no reason I can't tidy up more."

"I wrote a page today! If I keep that up, I could write a book someday."

"I can do two pushups now, and I couldn't do any before. I can get in shape if I keep working at it."

Tip #3. Pounce on your productive impulses!

If you're sitting somewhere and you think, "Hmm, I'd like to write____." Or, "I should rearrange my books." Don't let other tasks stop you. Do it while you feel inspired. By nature, even if you remember later, you won't want to as much as you do when it comes to you spontaneously.

In the same vein, when that little voice says, "I should shower…" The sooner you begin, the less time is available for you to possibly talk yourself out of it.

Tip #4. Just start.

Procrastination is my bane, and it is inherently tied to a belief in free will. Anyone can quit procrastinating. As we mentioned, it just means building trust in our intentions. Don't do anything at some unspecified "later." Do, or do not. Plan, but do not put off. Building trust in your own word means that you can begin to say, "Ah, I'll do that tonight" and know that it will be done.

Try this:

Pick one thing to do in the next hour. Make it reasonable enough for you.

Write it down here.

_____

You picked something? Now trust me and trust yourself.
Start now. Put this book down and do that thing.
It's your mission.
This is proof that you can quit procrastinating. Work steadily and commit to doing things now, if they truly need doing. Keep picking small things. Keep proving yourself. It'll be easier soon, I promise.

CHAPTER 2

Don't be so hard on yourself.

I f I had to describe how depression made me feel in four words, I'd say *unwelcome in my mind*. That was the primary sensation. That's why it was different from just being sad. Day in, day out, I was bullying myself. I was under constant attack. Of course I was tired! Of course I broke down! Of course I was numb, hopeless, and angry! How would you feel about a friend who makes jokes at your expense, puts you down when you fail, ignores your successes, and never thinks you're good enough?

That is exactly how I used to treat myself. It was always "Sorry I'm this, sorry I'm that." There are a hundred thousand ways to bully yourself with words.

All the little things added up. Criticism turned to hatred. Everything made me tired. Everything made me hate myself. The more I hated myself, the more tired I felt, and the more tired I felt, the further I fell. My grades slipped. When I spoke, I snapped. When I wasn't angry, I'd cry. I didn't notice how much my self-deprecation was affecting me. Slowly but surely, it became my status quo.

And how could I have noticed? That's how my friends talked about themselves. We made jokes at our own expense at lunch, on twitter, in the morning, before bed. You've seen the jokes, the posts, the fatalistic streak my generation has. It's a culture of fear and loathing. I hardly knew there was another way to exist.

I think everyone would like to have better self-esteem. I did, too, but I wanted it in the sort of far-off fantasy way that someone living paycheck-to-paycheck wants a cherry red Porsche. Wouldn't it be nice if I had better self-esteem?

But I found the secret. Words.

Whether it's a joke or not— whether they "really mean it" or not— when someone says something mean to you, doesn't it hurt?

A relationship doesn't go sour for no reason: it's the daily practice of talking to each other that forms how we feel. Compliments grow scarce; words of support are out the door. Every situation becomes an excuse to snipe at each other! Every problem is your fault.

No, your fault. *No, it's your fault.*

The same goes for what we say about ourselves. Every little comment matters. I changed the way I felt about myself by changing the way I talked about myself. It wasn't easy, but it was a measurable, achievable goal. That was more than I'd ever had before.

I did three things:
1. I stopped saying mean things about myself, full stop. Even jokes! And I loved a good self-deprecating joke.
2. Even when I couldn't believe them yet, I started saying positive affirmations instead.
3. Everything I said to or about myself came under the same scrutiny: The Friend Rule. If I wouldn't say it to my best friend, I don't say it to myself.

Somehow it worked. The words I spoke turned into the words I thought, and the words I thought turned into me. I went from just feigning self-respect to truly wanting to look out for myself. Like any relationship, it took time and work; it didn't happen overnight. And still, it's the foundation of my recovery. Every time I do something good for myself, I do it because I give a damn whether I am okay or not.

Actually giving a damn starts with the words you say to yourself, and eventually, this self-respect extends to actions. You start to improve your life. Kick addictions. Take care of yourself.

I know that for some blessed people, self-respect is automatic. I had to learn. My friends and family taught me how to love myself: not by telling me, "Ruby, you need to love yourself," but by showing me what acceptance feels like. I always knew how to treat others with basic decency, and I knew what standard to expect from strangers and pals. I just had to apply that same standard to my inner life.

Being a friend to yourself means cutting yourself the same slack you already give to others. It means recognizing setbacks, celebrating progress, and forgiving mistakes. It means making a conscious effort to speak kindly and show respect. And most of all, it means pushing through, even when all you want is to sink down. By changing the words I used, I became my own best friend. I keep my successes folded carefully in my heart. I wipe my own eyes when the world is too much to handle. And you know what?

STORYTIME:
THE MORE UNSUSTAINED.

Going to camp was an *enormous* privilege which I coveted and counted down to by the day. *365. 228. 54. 3. 2. 1.*

Because I'd scored well on the SAT in 7th grade, I was invited to pay lots of money to take one college-level class of my choosing at various universities as part of the Duke University Talent Identification Program. So, I came home every year with six new best friends whom I'd die for, an intense and deep knowledge of jazz scales or Henri Matisse, and a complete inability to shut up about any of it.

I was further indoctrinated into loving Duke TIP by a slew of traditions and rituals that we all performed with the utmost seriousness. It was a little cult-y, but that was the fun part. "Mom, Mom," I raved, "It started out as a llama piñata, but someone's dad was a doctor, so they got it cast in resin. It's someone's job to carry it around at all times. The Llama [Pronounce: Ya-mah] is fifteen years old now; I hear if you kiss its forehead, you have good luck for seven days!"

Even my confusing, lonely post-dropout world of spiraling self-hatred couldn't bleach the Camp Spirit out of me. Like years before, I counted down the days. I took a plane to North Carolina by myself. I looked at the dewy green quads and the best friends I'd missed all year and I thought again and again how lucky I was that my family could afford this. A lifetime passed in the three-week pocket dimension that was Camp.

The ride was almost over. It was time to be named.

I looped my leg over where the chair attached to my desk and let the door swing closed with a deafening "KA-CHUNK." My ears burned white hot. *They're talking about me, I can feel it.* As if in an earthquake, tiles once-square warped and rippled into that whirlpool door. Closed and hiding terrible secrets, I never wanted it to open.

For the end of the year camp "yearbook", every member of every class broke off one by one to be named "most." "Most likely to kill Thomas Jefferson," "Most likely to win a Grammy," "Most likely to nurse baby birds back to health and cry when they fly free."

I was the last one up alphabetically: normal for a Walker, but nerve wracking every time. I hummed to myself while I waited. If I was humming, I couldn't hear. And if I couldn't hear, this was not happening.

I didn't want them to think about me. It was the same reason I avoided pictures: I hated seeing myself through someone else's eyes. Classmates and cameras weren't sensitive to my insecurities. There was no room to ignore things. A camera didn't care that it showed my asymmetrical face or the zit on my nose. Classmates didn't know that when they told me I was loud, I heard what I'd told myself a hundred times: "You have nothing good to say anyway, so why don't you just shut up?" People had no idea that when they said anything to me, anything at all, it just reminded me of everything I detested about myself.

My classroom door, that wooden gate to the inferno, clicked open mildly, and I was pulled from my anxious reverie. Roberto invited me back inside. Sixteen other teenagers gave me hopeful, expectant smiles while they revealed their choice.

RUBY: MOST LIKELY TO MARX.

Tears stung through the mild sunburn I'd had all summer. I didn't even *like* Marx that much! I just happened to have read about historical materialism before we discussed it in the first week. I hate being categorized, photographed— knowing what I was like to a stranger. I cried because the whole class, through all our discussions, I'd felt so raw and and blabbering and vulnerable. I read them poetry! Here were sixteen people who listened to every bit of that, and they still knew absolutely *nothing* about me. *How can anyone ever know me now?*

I put my head down on the desk and wet my forearms in an attempt to hide my shame; crying in class was old hat.

David scrunched his thick, grumpy eyebrows together. He looked like a muppet. "If you don't like it, we can try again," he said.

"No, I'm just- just being an idiot." A snake of a cold breath coiled in my lungs, poised to strike into some pathetic sob. I held my breath; I strangled it down. If I could just hide my face and control my voice—

Come on. Think of something. Say you like it. "I just thought about all the orphan babies who don't get cuddled."

"As long as you're okay," Bailey said. She was so nice. They all were.

Finally, the class marched out for supper. Light swung in low from the windows. I picked my head up from the table. The room had been tense, I felt— my unexpected tears bringing its teeth to my neck. I couldn't move until the moment was through. Alone in the room, I was released from its jaws. I crossed the quad and floated to my dorm: 212 Pegram hall.

The dorms were small. Just big enough for two beds, an up-right fan, and a strip of floor to stand on. I was still crying in full force— I couldn't let my roommate Kate see. She was so *wholesome* and *Christian* and *Arkansas*. Plus, I was pretty sure she'd heard me crying the night before. She'd report me to the administration for being so unstable. Under the covers, maybe?

I heard voices from down the hall, laughter and the *patpatpat* of trainers on thinning carpet. The time to make smart decisions was over— After everything, all I wanted was to be alone. I tucked my body under my two jackets in the back of the closet and shut myself away from the light.

So it was official: after years of searching and exploration, I had finally found a place to cry that was sadder than a bathroom stall. It smelled like old building. The hardwood floor creaked and groaned. A sliver of light touched only the tips of my toes. Soon everyone else left for dinner, and the only sounds were my stuttering breath and the ambient whir of that little fan. *Please, please don't let me get any worse than this.*

I tried to tug on my hair. Even that was a bust: I'd cut it all off in a fit of nihilism. There wasn't even enough to get a grip.

That one tiny frustration turned the tide on my self-pity.

God, this isn't working! And I don't just mean the stupid hair! I'm tired. I'm so tired. I thought things would be better here. My parents paid so much to send me here. I wan ted everything to be like it was last year. I wanted to be happy. I came all the way here so I could be happy. Why am I not happy? This is exactly like school was. This is exactly like home was. I spent last night considering getting drunk off Purell. I googled how to do it! It's just… The same! I'm in another state and it's the same, I'm so tired. I'm just. So. Tired.

My mind flicked to Sylvia Plath, Virginia Woolf, Vincent Van Gogh, and the kid from my 6th grade class who offed himself in a closet like this. He was twelve. Was that how I wanted to end up? Was I going to make myself feel this wretched no matter where I went?

The ticking of my watch was a physical pain— 6:20PM. I had lost my chance at grabbing a quick dinner. Soon they'd see I was missing from evening activities— In a daze of anger, I left the closet and left the room.

That summer, I decided to take my mother's advice. Ignoring good advice always takes a certain amount of arrogance: my whole life I'd heard, "Don't be so hard on yourself." But I didn't feel like changing. No, I thought I was doing just fine without yoga-practicing hippies butting into my business.

But what I was doing was not working. If you smell crap wherever you go, it might be time to check under your own heel. The way I was treating myself was making me miserable— and I could either do something about that, or I could keep crying into my elbows.

Like breathing out after too long, I had an unassuming little thought.

I really ought to try being kind to myself.

This was easier said than done. I mean, it isn't like there's a switch somewhere that I could easily flick to gain self-respect. I was tired of hearing about it.

But I *could* control the way I spoke about myself. Even if I didn't believe the things I was saying, I was so desperate to feel even a little bit better that I could handle lying through my teeth. Since I still couldn't even imagine expelling self-hatred from my mind, all I needed to do was keep it out of my mouth. For the next week, every time I caught myself about to mutter, "I'm an idiot," I would say the opposite— "I'm a genius" — instead. I knew I didn't mean it, but oddly enough, I felt a little better.

All these revelations in mind, one day my class filed into the dungeon. Two stories below the Duke University library was a room, filled with gray rolling shelves, heaped to the throat with well-cataloged books. It was tomb silent. I chose my place at the far end of a long, skinny table and began marking down my copy of *The Culture Industry* by Horkheimer and Adorno.

First: The text itself was as predictably depressing as the work of two highly intelligent exiled German communist Jews in the '40s could be.

Second: I didn't know many of the words. What did firmament mean? Asceticism? And what in Sam Hill was "the Wagnerian dream of the *Gesamtkunstwerk*"?

Third, to send my compounding stress over the final edge: After twenty minutes, my classmates were already leaving the room to join in discussion— while I was only halfway through.

I underlined recklessly, rendering some words illegible. Blue ink bled through the pages of the essay and blotched on the side of my hands. When the last of my classmates left me, I started to skim ahead. The words slid untranslated off my eyes and gathered as a fog around my understanding. Then the last page: crystal clear. I was near tears again— not because I hadn't understood the meaning of what I read, but because I had, and it frightened me. Was so much of life lived only in service of an easy dollar?

I stumbled into the dim discussion room. Eyes bored into me. When I could have said, "I'm so dumb I could barely finish," I twisted the idea in my mind until it stopped pinching my anxious nerves. Instead I mumbled, "Sorry, I got really into it."

I didn't have to apologize. Three classmates were already sniffling in the left corner. I sat near them and felt alright when Emily handed me a tissue for my drizzling nose. There is something therapeutic about not being the only one crying like a baby. We lobbed dramatic accusations at Professor Niemczyk and hiccuped about how depressed *The Culture Industry* had made us.

That day at lunch, we huddled in the shade of a young tree and whispered furiously about what we'd learned. And then we moved on. We read Plato, Whitman, Anzaldúa, and Ginsberg. I finally felt close to my peers. I finally felt understood. We had the kind of bond that only forms through small dosages of shared suffering. I felt absolute.

We all went home, scattered around the country. The feeling drained away like a flattening tire.

All that time, when I felt so lost, I was looking for someone to care about me. The more I hated myself, the more I depended on others to make me feel okay. There was a hole in my heart—a lone-liness I couldn't shake. But the more sympathy I got, the more I felt ashamed.

Nobody else could fill that hole. Being understood by others feels amazing! It was so perfect I could almost forget it was fleeting. No matter how good I was, no matter how much I pleaded for it, or worked for it, I could never make everyone understand me. If my self-esteem was dependent on other people's feelings, it would never be under control. I'd be on a ship rocking back and forth between emptiness and salvation, never able to really find my feet.

And I knew that I'd never be able to love other people the way they deserved if I was always needing them, using them to make myself feel okay.

So I threw myself into the project of getting better.

I spoke the things I wanted into the world.

"Everyone makes mistakes."

"I'm going to be okay."

"Wow, I love being alive."

"I am a true artist."

"My friends love me."

"I love myself."

At night I'd stand in front of the mirror, eyes closed, imagining the face of a beloved friend. *Upturned nose, wavy hair, dark eyes, wide smile, belly laughing, lifting eyebrows, skipping stones.* I'd feel the cham-pagne glow of love and respect radiating from behind my sternum. When my eyes broke open on my own hateful face, I squeezed the embers tight to keep them from fizzling out. I kept forcing myself to imagine feeling self-love.

Then one night when I opened my eyes, I didn't see a ghoul or a failure or a mask. I saw a tired, imperfect girl who wanted the world to be kind.

And the love was already there.

> "*I* care for myself. The more solitary, the more friendless, the more unsustained I am, the more I will respect myself."
> — Charlotte Brontë, *Jane Eyre*

ADVICE ON HOW TO STOP THE HATE, GET SMART, AND TREAT YOURSELF RIGHT:

Tip #1. Make some records. If you're inclined to make negative comments about yourself, try writing down how often you do it. Just go through a normal day and keep a tally in felt marker on your wrist.

Is it a lot? Or maybe just a little. Now, consider for a moment if you would say those things about a close friend.

Tip #2. Ditch the sad jokes! I always thought my jokes were funny because they were self-deprecating. It turns out, they were funny because I was *overreacting*. Now when I hear someone making self-deprecating jokes, I just feel a twinge of sadness for them. You can still be funny without saying negative things about yourself!

When you catch yourself saying something unkind, just turn it around. You can even be sarcastic if you want. If you can flip the comment or joke before it leaves your mouth, even better.

Sad Joke	Funny Joke
I'm the worst person alive.	I was born this amazing.
I'm gonna kill myself.	I'm gonna assassinate the president.
I love death and dying.	I love life and living.
My painting looks like barf.	Somebody call the MOMA!
I'd drop dead if I tried running.	Usain Bolt can't touch me!
I only have two brain cells left.	My IQ and my SAT score are both 1700.

Tip #3. Breathe deep and forgive yourself. My mother taught me the very first anxiety fighting technique I ever learned, and I still use it to this day. It's self-comforting. Here is the technique as she showed me:

- Tap your collar or forehead rhythmically, taking slow, even breaths.
- Repeat the words: "Even though [bad thing.]" (e.g. "even though my dog is lost, and it's my fault, and she might be dead—"
- Take a very deep breath. Imagine taking in all that hate, grief and worry.
- Breathe it out. Imagine the worry leaving you.
- *"It's okay. I'm okay. And I truly, deeply love and respect myself."*

Tip #4. Say it, then believe it. These are the simple kinds of affirmations. If you don't believe them, close your eyes and say them anyway. Imagine saying kind words about someone you love. Keep some of that feeling and imagine feeling that way about yourself. Some of my favorites:

- I can love and forgive, just as I am loved and forgiven.
- I love myself.
- I'm okay. I'm gonna be okay.
- My future holds moments of joy I can't imagine yet.
- I deserve to be respected as I respect others.
- Life is a mixed bag, and my life contains possibility.
- My imperfections make me a unique and lovable person.
- I am profoundly lovable. I am capable of uncomplicated love.
- I am capable, talented, and kind.
- Life is good and it's good to be living.
- I know who I am, yet I am always growing and developing.
- I deserve the same kindness I automatically give to others.

When I started saying these things, I felt very odd standing alone and talking to myself. I promise, if affirmations work for you, it's totally worth feeling weird for a couple of minutes every day.

Tip #5. Try situational affirmations. These are more tied to optimistic hopes for certain circumstances.

- It's gonna be a great day.
- This bath is going to be so relaxing.
- First days are wonderful opportunities to make new friends.
- I studied my best and this test will be a breeze.
- Even if I don't get this job, I am a capable and good person.
- I'll complete this lab quickly and without distraction, because I am an intelligent and capable chemist.

Tip #6. Be aware of your thoughts.

Now that you're comfortable noticing and redirecting the things you say about yourself, it's a good time to consider what you're thinking about yourself. The practice you've gotten with spoken words can be useful when you want to change your thinking.

Tally again: How many times a day do you think self-critically? Would you say all these things to your best friend?

It takes practice, but once I could see how I was *saying* bad things about myself, I could also confront the fact that I was *thinking* bad things about myself. Two years later, I still have to remind myself all the time, "Don't beat yourself up!"

Say I've done badly on a test I didn't study very hard for. I'll start having thoughts like,

"I'm such a lazy asshole. Why didn't I study more? I'm gonna mess up my GPA, and I'll never get into university."

Then my friend-brain will kick in. I think, *what would I say to a friend who was having these problems?* How can I think of this in a positive way? How can I make sure I'm not needlessly beating myself up? Will these thoughts help or hurt me in achieving my goals?

Throughout the day, every day, I am doing a mini version of this in my head. When I catch myself dipping into negativity, I try my best to think uplifting things. If I'd like to be a good writer, it's *more useful* for me to research editing tips than it is to sit and stew about how awful I think my draft is.

Tip #7. Write it down!

Sometimes I can't organize my thoughts very well. I'm thinking five terrifying things at once, or I'm crying, and it's all overwhelming me. When this happens, I write down my problem. I complain a little. This helps me confront the voice in my head as a tangible thing.

And then I muster up the courage to reply, and I think:
What would the best version of myself say to this?
What would I say to a friend?
How can I solve this?
How can I be kind?

CHAPTER 3

Just get out there!

You probably need to exercise. I know! I know how it sounds. I'm not some sort of protein-guzzling gym rat who thinks forty push-ups can cure the clap, okay? *I swear.* I didn't start exercising until after I dropped out of high school. I never saw myself as a sporty person. All the people who didn't like me liked sports, so I just assumed it was a no-go.

That's the way they divide us up in school.

You're either a jock or a nerd, with no in-between. There was never a league for kids who wanted to be *alright* at volleyball.

If you weren't at least willing to get up at 6:30 for junior varsity athletics by middle school, your fate as a sedentary know-nothing was practically sealed. So, because of our school's incredible PR fumble, the fact that everyone needs physical activity to produce the right brain chemicals to function wasn't ever really instilled in my clique. Exercise was for the kids who were already strong, co-ordinated, and pretty. We had no business even trying.

I have come to understand that appearance and competition have nothing to do with the real benefits of exercise. There will always be someone taller, more muscular, faster, stronger, and with a lower body fat percentage than you. Forget about them. You and I need those zumba classes for a different reason:

When my mother told me exercise can work better than drugs, I gave her an odd look. She's the kind of mom who will give you herbs to cure a cold, and I was understandably skeptical of the whole procedure. Let's get serious:

Aerobic exercise is one of the most effective treatments for Major Depressive Disorder.

Compared to antidepressants, patients in clinical trials experience comparable results with moderate exercise. Plus, the rate of relapse (that is, patience whose depression returned within 12 weeks) was significantly lower in patients who either exercised alone or exercised in combination with antidepressants.

It's long-term, helpful in physical health, effective in mood treatment, and free if you don't buy equipment. The *only* drawback I can think of is possible injury. (It's advisable to talk to your doctor before starting any kind of fitness program.) Five million benefits and one tiny risk— sounds fantastic, right?

The hard part is starting out.

I mean, honestly, we've *all* heard that exercise is good. Good for sleep, sex, digestion, mood, blood, bones, fighting vampires, Buddhist enlightenment— you name it. And people don't *care*. That's the frustrating thing! It's the most amazing/fantastic/life-changing/world-affirming/endorphin-blasting hobby ever, and it is *ulcer-inducingly boring* to everyone but you.

Nobody ever cares how much you ran yesterday. They weren't there for the self-doubt, the pain, the triumph, the absolution. All they know is exactly how many feet of straight asphalt road you dripped stress sweat onto while wheeze-snorting like a geriatric pug. Having that conversation does nothing for them.

Imagine there's a drink. The Drink. And it's a really, really, *really* acquired taste.

"Ugh," you say, "Look at that girl. She's drinking The Drink. I don't know how some people can stand that."

For the first, say, month you drink it, executives at The Drink Company personally send a goon squad into your home to put scorpions in all your shoes, and maybe waterboard you a little. It also tastes like rancid rat piss that's been fermenting in a barrel made of wood from torn-down orphanages.

But yet— after that month! Something changes. Slowly, and then all at once, you start to like The Drink. It tastes like ethically sourced, fresh California oranges, and it tastes like the concept of true love. When you drink this Drink, everything feels okay, and right, and good, and you aren't even drunk! You just feel amazing. Opposite from destroying your liver, this drink strengthens your bones and decreases your risk of cancer. You keep trying to explain to your friends, "Yes, it tastes like rat piss. But. My bones! Look at my bones!"

Frankly, they think you're nuts, and a bit annoying. "You must just be one of those people who likes the taste of rat piss," they scoff. You try to explain that it gets better, but your encouragements fall on deaf ears. You've become the piss-drinker you once decried, and now there is no way for you to communicate with the non-Drink-drinkers you used to hold dear.

That's how it feels to say what I'm about to say.

STORYTIME:
I HATED EVERY MINUTE.

Twenty-three pairs of tiny sneakers squealed when they hit the wax-shiny floor of the Horn Elementary gymnasium. "Hey," a girl I knew, Aly, nudged me, "You actually, really never did this before?"

"We didn't have tests at my old school," I said, shuffling behind the red line and towards the windows that barely let light in. "We did like, acro-yoga? And the P.E. teacher Michael tried to teach everyone this dancey fighty thing, but I wasn't very good at it."

"Oh! That's so—"

Aly didn't get to finish the thought, because Coach Knell was booming from the stage at the side of the gym. "Toes behind the red line! I see you, Jackson, you can't sneak out. Y'all are too loud. Just do your best, kids, and after this we have the trunk lift."

She clicked a few times on a laptop. A disembodied voice filled the room.

"The FitnessGram Pacer Test is a multistage aerobic capacity test that progressively gets more difficult as it continues…"

I tugged my pink socks up above my knees, almost high enough to brush the hem of my khaki uniform skort. Then I tugged them up again. Jitters spread from my fingertips to fizz behind esophagus. When I heard that first ding, I shot off in a throng of classmates.

After only a few minutes, my lungs started to burn. It was time to stop.

No.

I want to pass this. The other kids aren't even tired. I need to make it.

I barely got to the other side of the gym before I heard another ding. I turned, swaying like a drunk, and used that momentum to fall into frantic step. I was running out of air. *It's supposed to be hard, I can do this, I can-*

Oh no, oh no, oh crap. A vignette of undulating black spots closed in on my vision. I heaved my chest, forcing my rib cage open. It felt like the air came through a coffee straw. I collapsed by the stage.

In. Out. In. Out. *Why am I so loud?*

If I breathed any quieter, though, I'd stop getting air entirely. It felt like someone filled my lungs with epoxy. Every time I wheezed, it got harder, squeezing out the last of my shallow breath. Eventually I got control of myself. I did the trunk lift. My family didn't think much of it until we all got sick, and I started to wheeze again.

"Reactive what?" I kicked my legs over the edge of the doctor's table. Dr. Auden slid the stethoscope's freezing probe down the left side of my spine. "Reactive airway disease," He said, "Slow breath in... that's good. Now breathe out."

I felt the infection purring through my bronchi. The rumbling mucus sound kept on for a few moments after I stopped pushing. I held onto the table, dizzy.

Dr. Auden ran more tests while Mom told him about every

lung problem I'd had since infancy. He swabbed my throat for strep. He made me blow into a tube. The meter fluttered up and sank quickly. He took an X-ray of my chest.

At the end of the visit, I knew five things:
1. I suck at running.
2. I have asthma.
3. I have bronchitis again.
4. I have to take a steroid inhaler twice a day.
5. The inhaler might stunt my growth a bit.

The rest of the year wasn't so bad. I actually did fine in P.E. I learned to square dance and roller skate. I just stopped running. I wasn't sure how much would trigger another attack, so I took naps 'till the end of recess while my classmates rocketed through the hissing dry grass around me.

Then, when I was twelve years old, I read a comic by Matthew Inman (pseudonym The Oatmeal) titled "The Terrible and Wonderful Reasons Why I Run Long Distance." You could probably still find it online. "It was on this day," Inman wrote, "During this terrible and wonderful run, that a thought occurred to me... I've always considered *the* question to be, 'Why am I alive? Why am I here? What's the point of me?' And to that I say: Who cares! Forget the *why*. You are in a raging forest full of beauty and agony and *magical grapey beverages* and *lightning storms* and *demon bees*. This is better than the *why*."

He wrote, "I run because I seek that clarity."

And so I started running the same week I read that comic, in the exact wrong shoes, with the exact wrong form, because I'd never had a moment so pristine. The Oatmeal put physical activity into a light I'd never seen before: it wasn't about being good enough, or beating my classmates, or being born with talent. At my school, you either scorned every variation of physical activity, or you were running miles in the morning, representing the Dahlstrom Mustangs, and bussing to competitions every weekend. The Oatmeal wasn't a perfect jock— he was just like me. He probably ate too many Oreo's, hated the sun, and drew funny things in the margins of his math notes.

This comic framed running in a way I understood: It was a transaction between effort and peace. Suffer for an hour or two every week and you, too, can silence everything but the visceral awareness of *how much sweat is pooling against the small of your back.* Some silence would be nice.

Of course, the suffering itself wasn't always so easy.

I started slow. I would've run a fifteen-minute mile, if I *could* run for fifteen entire minutes. I could barely run sixty seconds before my trachea rose up in mutiny.

"I'm training for a 5k," I said.

"Oh? Which one?" Mom said.

"I dunno, but I should be able to do it in six more weeks."

I caught strep throat and quit at one month. I just lost motivation after half a week. Too many holidays, two weeks. Shipped off to summer camp, five weeks. Influenza, three weeks. Thunderstorms, two and a half.

Every time I quit, my excuses got thinner. I did want to run a 5k. I just didn't want to *run*. My throat would burn in that telltale way after five minutes, and my stomach would stop, drop, and roll. I wasn't finding *clarity;* my feet just ached. Every time I started again at week one, I did so carrying an uncomfortable weight of dread: *wouldn't this be just like last time, and before that, and before that?* I took long breaks. Years, sometimes. But I never stopped trying.

I know how and when and why I started running. That much is clear— I also know how I got pretty good at it. The individual stories aren't interesting at all, just an endless repeat of, "I didn't wanna run, but then I did, and it was hard, but I was proud of myself," with different weather events inserted in for backdrop.

The more interesting question is this:
When did I start to *like* running?

I don't enjoy every run. Sometimes all I can feel is the tension in my ankles, and every step takes conscious effort. I keep checking my phone: five minutes left. I leap over bridges, slog through a marsh, see birds flying, get a cramp, lose the cramp, listen to an entire Kendrick album, and see the secrets of creation carved into the laboring spine of the last wild bison.

When I look back down at my watch, I have four minutes and fifty-five seconds left.

But some runs? Some runs I've started to *like*. Not just what they do for me, not just the idea of getting better at something, or a fetish for moving forward— I have started to enjoy the physical sensations of running. I love feeling like a furnace tearing through rain in the winter; I love the thump of my feet lining up with some disco song; and I love the burn of well-earned satisfaction, muscles still twitching, when all is said and done.

"I hated every minute of training, but I said, 'Don't quit. Suffer now and live the rest of your life as a champion.'"
— Muhammad Ali

ADVICE ON HOW TO START EXERCISING, DRINK RAT PISS, AND FIX YOUR BRAIN CHEMISTRY:

Tip #1. Just start, even if it's pathetic how little you're doing. Take a walk to the lamp post and back every night — No shame as long as you're doing something! In fact, just leave shame at the door— when we begin to exercise, we might go in as patent lawyers, slackers, single moms, dishwashers, washouts, dropouts or CEO's.... But we all come out the same way: ugly and sweaty.

Tip #2. Start with nothing. There's a trap so many people fall into, and here's the truth: Every company will try to hawk you some magic shake or shoe or program, but there is nothing you can buy that will make the hard parts of exercise easy. Sweat is unavoidable if it's hot and you're trying. Sore muscles become strong muscles. Thinking equipment (or a gym membership) is needed to start is very wrong. That's how gyms make money! If 100 people pay, and only 25 show up to use the weights, that's major profits. When I was a true beginner, I could barely use the lightest weights in the room. And all those buff dudes doing curls just intimidated and discouraged me.

Equipment can be helpful, but I didn't need it to start. I didn't need shake weights, a treadmill, fancy clothing, a plan, a schedule, or any earthly idea of what I was doing with myself. I just started... Stopped for a bit, but kept going. I didn't give up— I just took very long breaks. You can't really give a good thing up 'til you're dead. If it's right, you'll come back.

Without further ado, here are ten (almost) no-equipment exercises:

- Dance around.
- Lift a friend.
- Squats.
- Jumping Jacks.
- Walk (dog optional.)
- Swim.
- Jog.
- Push-ups (or halfsies.)
- Punch a pillow!
- Play ball.

You should ideally be getting a delicious pie chart of weight training, cardio, and stretching. But that's just for body health— you can get those sweet endorphins by jogwalking three times a week. I really recommend the couch to 5k program or any of its knockoffs!

Tip #4. Keep it up!

Making sure you continue to exercise after you've begun relies on two main principles: interest and variety. Everything is going to be hard at first. Everything is going to feel pretty bad. Keep in mind, you shouldn't be in huge pain, but it'll just... suck. And you'll suck at it. That's the #HardTruth.

So pick something you can see yourself loving after the "oh no, I'm sweating" phase is over. I picked biking, because I love the feeling of coasting down a hill. Then I picked running, because I'm a junkie for improvement. And it's easy to improve something you *royally suck* at. Keep picking things!

Tip #5. Recruit someone to help you stay on track! It
could be a friend, a relative, a sweetheart, or even just a pet who relies on you to take them out. Ultimately, exercise will benefit *you* the most... But buddying up is a great incentive to keep going.

My parents started walking the dogs together this year, early in the mornings before work. It's a very symbiotic activity. Mom is a people pleaser through and through— she went from being a film producer to a senior home care administrator, all while raising two kids. My stepdad Sean... mostly does his own thing, actually. He's an artist who likes to make cannibal jokes. They're both pushy people. They like to take care of everyone's problems but their own. So I hear them in the morning sometimes.

Mom: I stayed up too late last night...
Sean: Me too, lady. What's the point you wanna make?
Mom: Do you think poor Yahtzee can survive one day without us?
Mom and Sean: [Clinking dog leashes and complaining to each other]

I don't think Mom would go without Sean to nag her. And I don't think Sean would go without Mom to nag. It's good for them.

In the end, not everyone will get around to loving exercise, but I firmly believe that everyone loves *having already exercised*. It's a distinctly tired-happy-accomplished feeling. And all it takes to get from one to the other is a little sweat, and a little time. Take the first step with me, okay?

CHAPTER 4

Follow your dreams!

I had the confidence. I had the gumption. I could do any basic task I set out to do, and it felt like a superpower. People who have never dealt with mental illness will never understand know how legitimately triumphant it feels to *decide to take a shower* and then *actually do it*.

At this point I was really good at doing one step things, but I had no idea how to do more complicated stuff. I didn't even know what I *wanted* to do. It's hard to be okay when you feel like you're drifting away from things.

Didn't I think stuff was important before I was depressed? Didn't I have things I wanted to accomplish?

I wanted to find true love.

I wanted to be an actor.

I wanted to get rich.

I wanted to write screenplays.

When I *did* have ideas about what I wanted to do, they seemed so far off it was almost impossible to imagine actually doing them. This one isn't that hard once you get the basic premise.

Here's my extremely obvious advice: You need goals, and you need to figure out how to achieve them *bit by bit*. Every time I followed through with a goal, even if it was just to do three push-ups, I felt a little more confident. That made bigger things seem possible for the first time in a very long time.

Set specific goals, make a realistic plan to achieve them, and you will. You can and you will.

STORYTIME: STRENGTH, COURAGE, AND CONFIDENCE.

How do you go about writing a book? How can I piece together my written thoughts into a world someone else can enter? How can I immortalize my most embarrassing moments?

It's a struggle between doubt and faith! I have to keep fooling myself into thinking people will care what I have to say. How could I stand it if someone sees the most vulnerable piece of me laid to paper and says, "Eh, I've read better." Imagining the reviews I'll get on *goodreads.com* nearly gives me the shakes. I'm only seventeen. I have no illusions. I hope I'm readable; I can only pray I might be good.

I wonder if this is worthwhile. I doubt my consequence. I am not a writer—in my mind, novelists and writers always belonged to a different class of human. *They* would know how to do this. Those endowed with the natural to skill put to pen to paper, or fingers to keys, do so with the ease and practice of a swan taking flight from still water.

THE AUTHOR'S BOOKSHELF

It's hard for me to focus. I find reasons to avoid sitting down with my laptop. When I can't put something into words, I skip right to pictograms. I overuse em dashes, and I can't stop describing the way my lungs feel in-scene, the way my breath is coming. I am preoccupied with myself— I use others like props, and at this point it's too late to start telling anything chronologically.

In other words: I'm no swan. I'm no duck. I'm a chicken.

But I'm still going to finish this stupid book.

Here's how I got here: lying in bed, doing mostly nothing, I made the sort of promise that's binding. (Not the sort you usually know you'll break when circumstances change— "I'm never falling in love again!" or, "I'll start waking up early next week…")

It was an undramatic moment of importance. Some moments are showy— an argument that breaks glass, or anything involving sunsets, fireflies, or flowers. They scream, "I'll be great for the cinema!" They cast themselves in a golden glow, they're striking, and they fall in line with romantic and artistic ideals of importance.

It's essential to know the difference between an interesting moment and an important one. In fiction it's very easy to always match these two up. But in real life, important thoughts can strike you at any time, with no regard for how you'll later write them into gripping scenes. It doesn't really take something dramatic happening to change yourself. You don't need to survive a shipwreck or solve a murder.

Sometimes important decisions arrive softly. And sadly, dramatic moments can pass without importance. I remember a tearful, loud, and desperate breakdown ended with me running out into the rain— riotous clouds obscured the dark edges of the trees, and I thought— *This has to be my turning point.*

It wasn't.

My "turning point" was not a quick pivot. It was a long, tedious, serpentine curve. Lasting recovery means changing a little bit every moment you're alive.

Writing this book has been its own entire challenge, one that began with a mundane promise on a normal night in bed— that I'd write an hour on weekdays, just for the summer. I'd see where that went. I'd see if I had anything to say. When I got up the next morning, my bones were powder.

Will I keep my promise? Am I doing this? Can I do this?

I sat down and charted my course on paper, with specificity. Every weekday that summer — that's Monday, Tuesday, Wednesday, Thursday, and Friday— I would sit somewhere outside or inside with my blue Pilot G2 pen and a pad of legal paper, and I would write a terrible first draft. I chose pen and paper because it would mean no erasing.

That first day, I sat outside on my ankles in a broken plastic lawn chair and I wrote my way in. I had to be alone with my thoughts for an hour— all day I bit skin off the inside of my cheeks, tasted iron, anticipating the plunge.

What if I can't think of anything to write?

"Okay. I reserved this hour to start writing a book about getting over depression. The idea is making me so anxious…

So how about I tackle it?

What was point A, and what is point B?"

In that moment, I knew what had to be done. I knew it would be difficult, but I knew how I would get to where I needed to be: all I had to do was write a path from A to B, in instructions, in stories, in ink. All I had to do was keep writing until it was finished. The only thing that ever stood between my mind full of ideas and a finished book was a mundane promise and a careful plan.

> "You gain strength, courage and confidence by every ex-
> perience in which you really stop to look fear in the face.
> You are able to say to yourself, 'I have lived through this
> horror. I can take the next thing that comes along.'"
> — Eleanor Roosevelt

ADVICE ON HOW TO KEEP LOW EXPECTATIONS, SET HIGH HOPES, AND MAKE A PLAN TO GET STUFF DONE:

Tip #1. Be proud of the progress you make. Even the little things are irrevocable.

My good friend Anna said to me, "I've changed this summer. I don't want to go back to who I was."

"Dearest friend," I replied, "I'm glad you don't. If you tried, you'd surely fail."

Tip #2. Set realistic goals. If you can do simple stuff, and you figure out the right order to do all that simple stuff in, and you *do it*, you can accomplish pretty much whatever you decide to do.

I hate unnecessary acronyms as much as you do, believe me. But SMART goals worked well for me! An effective goal is:

> **Specific:** describe exactly what you'll do. "I wanna get better at guitar" isn't specific. "I want to play *Wonderwall* at the talent show in June" is. You can't really attain vague goals, so they just end up making you sad in a blurry way that's hard to get rid of.
> **Measurable:** decide how you'll see progress. Are you taking pictures of your garden as it grows? Are you counting how many squats you do every week? Do you just want to see your test grades improve, or do you want to be able to explain Thermodynamics to a friend?
> **Achievable:** decide that you can.
> **Realistic:** work out logistics like money and travel. If you wanted to climb a certain mountain, do you know how long the drive there is? Do you have supplies?
> Timed: set a time frame and set aside time to work. When do you want to show your artwork? How long does it usually take you to paint something? How much time do you need to set aside for setup?

Here's an example of a few nice, simple goals I've had.

- I'll run on Wednesdays, Fridays, and Sundays— increasing the time a little each day. Then, next week on Monday, increase the time from 20 to 30 minutes.

- I have a paper due in Composition next Tuesday. I'll write an outline to get started— I know it needs to be 1500 words. If I write 300 words a day, I'll have a few days left over to revise and edit my draft. I'll start working at 4pm in the library today.

Tip #3. Link little goals to big goals.

Try this: get a piece of paper and fold it in thirds. Now, label the thirds "today" "this month" and "this year." Write down something you want to do and work backwards.

This time next year, I want a 4.0 GPA.

Pretty audacious! You can pick anything you like— that was the real goal I chose the first time I did this. If you decide there's something you want to do, it doesn't need to be a scary ordeal. Everything becomes more manageable when you break it down.

Think about your goal. "If I want to have a 4.0 GPA next year, what do I need to do in the next 4 months? The next month? Come up with the smaller components that feed into your big goal.

To get a 4.0, I'll need to be more organized, choose classes that fit me, and spend more time studying after school.

Then you simply come up with ways you can get started on those smaller goals today.

To get organized, I can start a planner and clear off my desk.

To study more, I can schedule dedicated time for it in my planner, and start highlighting my notes tonight.

To choose good classes, I can do some research on degreeMap and Rate My Professor in the library after class. I can also schedule an appointment with my school counselor.

This helps in two ways! One, large goals seem less daunting with a plan. They're achievable. And two, short goals are motivated by larger goals. Their importance is clear.

Tip #4. Keep a planner.

I didn't think I was the organized type! My spaces, including the inside of my head, were constantly a mess— so wasn't this my natural state?

Turns out I like being organized. I just don't like *organizing*. Or really, I didn't even know how to start. I'm still not a neat freak, but time management *is* stress management. Getting things done when I want them done takes the pressure off and lets me have fun jumping into the next task.

When I have a plan and I'm doing it right, I'm not utterly relaxed—nobody is— but instead of always scrambling, I feel like life is pitching at a pace I can hit.

I used to be pretty bad at remembering all those plans.. Checklists.. Dates… projects. I'd scrawl something ambitious down onto a legal pad, and because I wrote it down, that would feel like I actually did something. I'd bask in my smug afterglow. But then I'd forget my precious list in the pocket of someone else's jeans, and boom— I had less time, paper, motivation than when I started.

Here is how to get started using a planner:

Step 1. Procure a notebook.
Any notebook. You could get one with a calendar already printed, or could draw that on yourself. I got a regular composition book since I like to use things that I wouldn't feel bad about ruining. Some of my friends prefer to invest in nicer things. Just get something you think you'll use.

Step 2. What should you write inside?
Little notes, little goals. Whatever you think you'll need to remember or do—
"Math homework 3.4."
"I ate way too much shrimp for lunch!"
"Run and then stretch for 15 minutes."
"Nature boy— Miles Davis."

Now if you google planners, you'll see a lot of perfect hand-made layouts in six colors with stickers and line graphs and glitter. If you're crafty and you'd like to do that kind of thing, go ahead. But it isn't a requirement. A planner is just a bunch of notes on a calendar— you can stop using it for a few days, spill coffee on it, dedicate five pages to a playlist you made for a crush— whatever! To me, it's where all my wild dreams and complex plans come home to rest for the night. It's how I know they'll be there in the morning. Sometimes I only fill it out with crayons. Sometimes I skip a week or two.

Your life, your rules.

CHAPTER 5

Take some time to heal.

I'm no psychologist, so I can't explain the reason so many people who deal with trauma end up with depression, too. But we all know it's true. That's common sense, isn't it? I can't imagine a world where having terrible things happen to me would make me happier.

Sometimes I spend days wishing I could make the memories go away. I wish I could take a time machine back. I wish I could force it out of my mind. But the truth is, it's there, and I can't make the truth of my past go away, no matter how much I want to. What happened is a simple fact. Nothing can change that. This is my life.

And this may read to you like a declaration of resignation. Not so! As much as the past is fixed, the future is mutable. I do not make my circumstances; I make myself. What I have to do now is focus on the beliefs and thoughts that accompany my experience.

If I could send a message in a bottle to the scared little girl I was when I was fifteen, I would send her this:

FOUR LIES YOUR TRAUMA IS TELLING YOU, AND WHY YOU MUST NOT BELIEVE THEM:

ONE: "This was your fault."

You didn't ask to be hurt. You didn't 'walk right into it.' You weren't wearing the wrong thing, saying the wrong thing, being annoying, acting stuck-up. You weren't too trusting. You weren't too kind, too mean, too quiet, or too loud.

People want to blame the victims of awful things because they want to believe in a *just world*. They want to believe there's an order to this planet: that bad things happen to bad people, good things happen to good people, and that's that. I understand. Wouldn't that be a comforting thing to believe?

Our culture relies on this. In order to reconcile the way oppressed people are treated with their idea of a just world, people think, "Oh, well, she must have said something awful, to deserve getting hit." People think, "Oh, well, he must've been doing something threatening, if the cops stopped him in the first place." It's what happens when *the truth* is put into conflict with *what seems right*. And this myth is so pervasive, so all-consuming, that even the victims themselves start to believe in it. "Oh, well," I find myself thinking, before I can stop, "I should've run away. I should've screamed. I must've wanted it to go that way after all."

But here's the truth: bad people get really rich. Good people get cancer. Horrible, terrible things happen to people who've done absolutely nothing to deserve it. I can't fix it, and I can't make it make sense.

All we can do is try to be kind. All we can give each other is a fair chance. Someday I'd like to see that our culture has changed—that when someone's pushed down, our first thought isn't, "Gee, should've looked where she was going," it's, "Hey, do you need a hand getting up?"

YOU DESERVE TO BE ANGRY.
SAD.
HURT.
forgiven.
loved.
ABSOLVED.
HAPPY.

TWO: "You shouldn't be so hung up on this— it's all in your head."

The brain controls every function of life. It isn't "just in your head." It's in your *head*. Imagine being shot in with an arrow— would you call that 'only in your head?'

Don't treat psychic injuries like they don't need time and care to heal, just like physical injuries. Don't let anyone tell you to "just get over it." Don't let anyone tell you you're doing this for attention.

I've met so many people with really upsetting memories, memories that affect their lives still and make things very hard for them, who've been told that they're "doing it for attention."

First, the accusation is ridiculous on its face, because it's perfectly normal to want attention when you are hurt. It's also normal to want to be alone when you are hurt. It's normal to *react.* It's normal to not be okay all the time. It's normal to feel like you will never be okay.

And second, I have never met a single person who was truly "just doing it for the attention."

If something's happened to you, and you are in pain, you deserve to get the support and care required to manage this pain. **The best option is to see a mental health professional—** but you don't need an official diagnosis of PTSD to understand that you are struggling with traumatic events.

"ALL IN MY HEAD!"

THREE: "Nobody will understand. Nobody will care."

I had a friend in sixth grade named Casey. She said odd things sometimes. She didn't talk like someone who was ten years old last year— she talked like she was pushing fifty-five and divorced, with a lifetime of regrets. Or maybe like a 28-year-old New York ex-socialite reminiscing about her days pounding the dance floor and paying PAs under the table to fetch her more MDMA.

"Casey, you already had your first kiss?"

"I was a slutty kid," she said, and our lunch table laughed.

"Casey, how many boyfriends have you had?"

"I was a little whore," she said once, then repeatedly. It became one of those facts you learn about someone vaguely and then never examine. I knew she'd been around with boys— or a boy, somehow. I knew she didn't like to be touched. I knew these things, and I never asked about them. Years passed. We stayed friends, and I forgot about those jokes.

Then when we were seventeen, she told me. More details than I'll give you here.

"I was raped," she said, "But I don't remember how much."

"There's stuff I don't remember either," I said, knowing it didn't compare, knowing it could never be enough, "I'm so sorry."

"Me too."

Sometimes life's a shit boat, and it feels like nothing's ever gone right. And sometimes the only comfort you have is the fact that other people are also in your awful situation. And maybe, just maybe, you'll make them feel a little less alone.

People *will* understand. Once you open up to them, an uncomfortable amount of your friends and peers might open up to you. It's actually frightening how many people understand what you are going through, and it's maddening, the fact that these awful things happen so much. I can barely stand to think about it. If I asked a room full of my friends if they'd ever been assaulted or abused, it would be a sea of raised hands.

RAISE YOUR HAND IF...

You are hurt. You are scared. You are furious. All of this might be true. But as much as I hate to write it, because I wish the world were a different place— you must not think for a *second* that you are alone.

FOUR: "You are going to feel this wrecked forever."

Nothing lasts forever. You'll learn to stop doing things that make you feel worse. You'll figure out what makes it a little better— therapy, friendship, fury, forgiveness.

You'll blink and it'll be three years later, and you'll have weeks when it almost snaps your bones. You'll want to drink. You'll wake up in a sticky, nervous sweat from a nightmare that's all hands. Your brain will replay it without cue, like a curse. Dread will fill you in slow spoonfuls.

And then you will have your weeks, more of them each year, when you only think of it in passing, and you'll finally feel nothing. You'll never be glad it happened, never. But some days...

STORYTIME:
HOW WE DEAL WITH IT.

"_____-, make you."

I jerked myself away, but they were bigger— nine or ten when I was six or seven. A hand caught my arm above the elbow and squeezed. The boy pushed me down, folding my body into a deep hole.

Far back in the schoolyard where teacher supervision was sparse, we had a large plateau of coarse builder's sand to play in. The boy had brown crescents under his stubby nails from digging. The girl was only there to watch. I remember that: her round face, her long black hair, laughing down from over my head, like this game was such fun for everyone. I can't remember if they buried me completely.

I also can't remember what happened right after. I probably ran inside to rinse the sand out of my eyes, cutting the line to the water fountain, crying. A teacher must've helped me eventually, but I still felt the scratches, even when all the grit was gone.

A Sunday in February: I situated my laptop on my crossed legs and settled in to watch the documentary. It was one of those YouTube explorations. I was bored. I clicked on a shocking title. "America's Youngest Sex Offenders."

One of the stars of the documentary was a boy my age named Clutter. He turned my stomach. I saw footage of him talking on the phone, trying to spell on a dry-erase board, and making small talk to a friend. I saw how the makers of the documentary wanted him to appear: benign. They kept talking about him like he was getting better. But I couldn't shake the feeling that it was all a farce.

Don't you ever just get a feeling about someone?

He had a head of buzzed brown hair, an under bite, and milk-bottle glasses.

No. That wasn't right. He didn't wear glasses.

Caleb G. was called Caleb G. because there was a Caleb J. at our school whose last name was Jackson. Caleb J. was good at math. He told me his great grandpa invented the Bowie knife, but I didn't know what that was, so I just nodded and smiled. Caleb G. did things like waiting until I was alone to shove me into a hole and bury me in sand. He cut the straps on my sandals, put poison ivy in my backpack, and flipped up my skirt when I wore one. He hit me sometimes, but only when he could corner me somewhere alone. Mostly he just made me afraid that he'd hit me again.

All the adults told me, "He must have a crush on you, that's how boys are."

Caleb G. told me, "It's called a pussy. I wanna see yours."

Clutter reminded me of someone I used to know— mostly in his buzzed brown hair, and the way he spoke like he was deciding exactly how to make you believe him. Seeing that documentary made me think:

"Wait, can a kid do that to another kid?" "A little boy do that to a little girl?" and, "Didn't that happen to me?"

It wasn't as if I didn't know I had a bully when I was a kid, I just never thought about it. The memories had been there, waiting,

unexamined, unimportant, tiny and blurry in the very back of my mind. I just assumed every bully did things like that. A few times, I'd even told some of the stories as jokes. People laughed. It was *normal*. Right?

Something I'd always re-membered changed into some-thing ghastly in the light of my new understanding. Kids can hurt other kids. Just because he called it a game, doesn't mean it was a game.

68

I couldn't stop thinking about it. It wasn't the same! I mean, I barely remembered what happened. I was six. I was probably just twisting it in my head, remembering it wrong so it would fit what I was seeing on screen. I closed my laptop. I stopped watching. I got up, the ground solid under me, the world unchanged— but I felt rancid. I paced in the kitchen. My dog whined at me, rubbing her face on my jeans like she knew.

Sawdust-hot air filled with the sharp stench of urine. It pooled there, seeping into the seam between planks of bent plywood. I was in a small wooden playhouse with Caleb G. and some boys, their faces blurred. He stood in front of the door, laughing at me, holding his—

I didn't remember everything that happened. Some things were just flashes of sensations, images, smells. If it had bothered me so much, why didn't I tell anyone? It wasn't so bad. It can't have been so bad. I was overreacting. I knew millions of people had it worse than I did—I just wish that had made it hurt less. I wish that my tears didn't come so hard, when I let myself admit it, when I couldn't understand what was already sounding true: sexual assault. I felt guilty for even using the words in my own head. I was faking it, I was stealing those words. They were for people who really had it hard, I knew that, but there was no way to make myself un-believe it. He wasn't just a bully. He ruined me. He assaulted me. He—

He took me below the cottonwood tree behind the wood shop— or was it oak? He took me there. The spot was hidden behind a hill and and empty while the other kids ate lunch inside. I kept trying to convince him not to make me strip. It wasn't working. I should've just run away, or yelled, but he was faster and stronger than me, and I felt frozen under the threat of some nebulous revenge I knew he'd take. If I could just get through this, then nothing worse would happen.

"Take your pants off, I wanna see."

"It's a little butt." I said, "It looks the same in front as it does in the back!"

"No, I wanna see," He pressed. I didn't like it when we played this game. "Either pull down your panties and show me, or take off your shirt."

I could've laughed. My shirt? Just my shirt? There wasn't anything private about my chest. He was weird. I pulled it over my head, relieved. Then my memory turned to pale fog as he looked at me, all over.

I hated him. Eight years too late, I shook and cried and I hated him. Tucked between the toilet and the wall, the furthest place in the house from my parents' ears, I called the RAINN hotline.

"Hello, this is—"

Click. No. I hung up at once. The lady sounded like someone who was used to dealing with real problems, and that made me feel like an idiot. How could I take time away from people with more important issues? He never touched me, not like that. Not that I could remember. But there was so very little I could remember, most all of it lost to a blank white fog of childhood amnesia. What if something happened that I didn't remember? Did it matter? Why did I keep thinking about it? It was like I *wanted* someone to hurt me. No. I could handle this alone. I could handle this if the memories stopped hijacking my eyes.

His hand squeezing my wrist.
He grinned at me, and I hated what that meant.

I called RAINN again. I needed to talk to someone. My friends would think I was disgusting. My parents— oh Lord, no. Telling my stepdad would make it weird. Mom would think it was all her fault, and then she'd be crying too. RAINN routed me to a local organization.

"Hi, this is SAFE Austin and my name is José," said a young voice, and I decided after two split seconds that he sounded non-judgmental enough to trust with my dumb fake problems.

"I'm—" I sobbed, "I'm sorry, I'm sorry, I just," I sniffed, "Gimme a sec, I can't breathe right. This is stupid. I'm an idiot." I wiped the snot off my face with the back of my hand and it trailed onto my forearm.

"Hey, it's alright. Whenever you're ready, I'm here."

"Okay," I sniffed again, and hiccuped, and then I finally gasped in enough air for actual speech. "You gotta know first, I'm not... It's not top priority. It's been like eight years, so I don't even know why I'm crying now, but. I just. I'm not in danger or anything, I'm fine. I don't even know if this is for just talking, I'm really sorry."

"Something that happened in the past is upsetting you?"

"It's. Yeah," I said.

José started off so gentle, "You should know, this is all entirely confidential…"

The more I talked, the less I cried.

All the adults told me, "He just likes you."

José told me, "What he did wasn't okay, and it wasn't your fault."

In the crook of the roots of that big oak tree by the wood shop there was a fungus. Puffy and cream-colored, it was riddled with holes that oozed orange fluid. I'd always imagined that it would start to eat your skin if you stuck a finger in. I watched it grow, week by week, disgusted, fascinated. Later I would identify it as a weeping conk, but at age six I just knew I couldn't trust something that couldn't decide if it was a plant or an animal.

"Oh, gross, don't!"

Caleb G. used his bare foot to mash the fungus to an oozing pulp. Slowly. I squirmed.

"Go on," he said, "It's your turn."

"Please don't make me."

"Don't make me make you, then."

I crouched down and touched the fungus. That's how things worked: he told me to, and I did. The further my fingers sank into its brown flesh, the more I expected to feel some sting or tingle that would signal the dissolution of my hand. But it never burned. It was just wet.

When I was done, he leaned close like he was telling a secret. One hand was braced on the tree. The other had had his— and he was pulling on it. I didn't know why—was it something about the tree? Was it me? I just saw his hand, pulling, and he looked so angry, eyebrows contorted. Eventually he finished pulling. He might've said something about it. This was just another one of those things he did to make me feel frozen.

February ended as winter hesitantly flickered into spring. I snuck nonstick bandage pads from my mother's bathroom closet, and of course they didn't stick well enough, so I wore spandex shorts under my jeans to hold them in place on the outside of my thighs. My friends would be over soon. I wanted them to have a good time, and know that I was fine, and laugh with me— but it's strange, how much I also wanted them to notice. I didn't really *need* bandages. The cuts I made barely bled. I just wanted—

I pictured Alicia seeing the white peek out of my spandex. I wanted her to ask me, "Ruby, are you okay?" And I wanted to tell her, "No! I've been cutting, I've been drinking, I feel so unreal." I wanted to fall apart in public so it could finally be someone else's responsibility to pick me back up. I wanted someone to know me. I wanted someone to make me stop.

I wanted all that— but I couldn't stand the idea of letting someone else see how weak I was. That's how I sank so low, so quietly. I was trapped in dichotomy— certain of two things at once that couldn't possibly agree. Believing what happened wasn't bad enough to be so shaken over, but still coming undone. Blaming myself entirely, but still feeling powerless. Standing on the razor's edge, knowing that I was doing myself wrong, but falling back in every single time.

Why did I keep cutting myself? Should I count the clichés?
To feel something, maybe.
To know my body was mine to hurt, maybe.
To have a real reason to feel bad, maybe.
To do something completely unacceptable, maybe.
To take failing myself to spectacular new heights, maybe.
I could give any excuse.

The truth was, I didn't *know* why I kept hurting myself. In public I was managing to laugh and smile, but in private there were two of me: one who thought, and one who acted; one who felt, and one who condemned. I'd be outside my body, above my head, watching calmly as the frightened little girl on the ground made bad decision after bad decision.

My friends came over. We drank tea and slogged through thick mud to pet my neighbors' new baby goats. We had a good time. They didn't see anything. They didn't ask.

I quit cutting before the wildflowers covered the roadside that spring— Not only because it hurt me, but because it wasn't *working*.

It didn't make me feel more real, or more powerful. It wasn't cool or meaningful. It wasn't poetic. It made me feel weak and stupid.

A Tuesday in March: I was camping by a little lake with some friends for spring break, three girls and two guys. John came and sat next to me in the hammock, his mess of curly hair dripping water. We swung a bit.

"Done swimming?"

"Hours ago," he said, "I just had a shower, though." Then he put his heavy arm around me, and my insides turned to oversalted movie theater popcorn.

"Take off your shirt," he said. Amber in a tree's roots. Sand in my eyes. No.

I held still in the feeling. I froze and let the world happen to me. I could handle this much. I trusted my friends. Eventually my nerves settled down, uneasy but unpanicked. We cracked jokes and watched the clouds fly.

After a moment, my nosy friend Allen came by, said,

"Why don't you two just date?"

I jerked back like a hand on a hot stove top.

John laughed. "Come on," he said, "You made it weird!"
Maybe I would've wanted to date him — if this, if that, if only.

I wished I didn't need an ocean of space to feel comfortable. I still wanted to be loved. Yet again I felt like two people: one who desperately needed a hug, and one who would break apart at the slightest touch. How could I get people to keep their distance without leaving completely? How long would it take for them to get tired of the way I flinched and evaded?

When I woke up gasping in our tent the next morning, I lied to my friends, told them I couldn't remember the contents of my nightmares. There was no way to explain why I felt like prey.

A Wednesday in July: When decided I was done feeling broken, and summer turned the roadside grass golden-dry, I expected it all to go away. I turned past the big stone posts of the Elliott Ranch gate and entered a bowl-like neighborhood. The gated community next to my house was snobbish, well-maintained, and low in traffic: perfect for a meandering evening stroll. Turning right had me squinting into the not-quite-setting sun, so I banked left on a curving uphill road lined with St. Augustine grass and driveway basketball hoops.

I walked for quiet. I walked to feel like I was moving forward. I walked until the sky was all brass and lilac— the slant of light hitting the hair on my arms made me glow like an angel. I only liked my skin at sunset. The sun fell behind the trees, silhouetting them black, and I turned to float home under the light of a fading blue raspberry snow cone sky.

A sound behind me shattered the peace. Five or six boys I might've known in high school chattered as they made their way down the street, and my body went into lockdown again. I squeezed my knife until it stung the heel of my palm. I practiced compulsively, fitting my thumb into that laser cut circle in the blade. In, out, click, click. That boy with the sandy hair— if he grabbed me by the arm, could I twist free? If he held me down, could I stick this knife between his ribs? If he said something to me, could I make myself speak? My back went stiff, rigor mortis setting in early. Maybe if I went tense enough, I'd collapse into myself.

They'd hear a crunch.

They'd walk over.

They'd see the lump of coal that used to be me.

A quarter the size, but four times as dense.

Here's what really happened: five or six boys I might've known in high school passed me by with nothing but a friendly wave.

It was fine, though. I had a plan to get better. I'd learn to love myself, and I wouldn't think about it, and then one day I'd forget again, and I'd be okay like before. I didn't need to tell anybody. The less people knew about me, the stronger I'd be. I wouldn't give them *anything*.

A Thursday in September:

Sam and I lagged back behind the group, breaking secrets open and hiding them in our clasped hands. Amber streetlamps gave us light in dissected strands. Perfect darkness. Perfect privacy. Our friends were roaming a full light ahead of us

. "So then I gave him a blowjob, and he gave me sixty bucks, and that was it," he paused, "I'm sorry, my hand must be sweaty."

"I mean, I don't feel anything. I'm probably sweating too."

Sam and I weren't friends, somehow, but we were always at the edge of it. We operated on the same level and worked so well—which is why here and now, it was like we'd been friends for years, even if we never hung out.

"Did you like him?"

"No," he said.

I squeezed his wide palm tighter, like I could compact him down and keep him safe.

"I feel like… This guy, you know. I was molested. He took all my firsts anyway. So. What would I be protecting?"

What do you say to that? I wasn't happy he'd been hurt, but still my heart swelled. I was happy we were together, crossing the road, a streetlight back from John's birthday party. We weren't alone. I couldn't change what happened to him, but I could keep holding his hand. My heart pounded.

What if it wasn't bad enough? What if I'm a fake? What if he thinks I'm gross? What if—

As I worried, the silence dragged on a second too long. Sam laughed, "Sorry, that was kind of a weird thing to say—"

Augh! To Hell with doubts! Sam was more important than my issues. Once we crossed the next street, I got close enough to speak in a voice measured and quiet, "Me too. Some stuff happened to me too. You're not weird."

Then I hugged him, or he hugged me. He felt bony and warm in my arms. A car passed. Cicadas screamed in tune. Eventually we caught up with the party, and for the first time since I remembered it all, I think I felt something like peace.

> "Pain is important: how we evade it, how we succumb to it, how we deal with it, how we transcend it."
> — Audre Lorde

ADVICE ON HOW TO SLOW DOWN, SPEAK UP, AND SURVIVE THE WORST OF IT:

Tip #1. Talk and listen. As much as possible, people need to know that they aren't alone in the universe. It's hard to talk and write about. But if nobody tells, and nobody writes, then the people who hurt us will hurt us tenfold. All our hurt will be isolated. Trapped in our bodies, it multiplies and festers. Talking about it flushes out the wound.

- It is always a great idea to see a counselor or therapist. I will absolutely find one sometime; even now I know it's something I want to talk to a professional about.
- Telling a friend can seem insurmountably scary, but it can be worth the nerves.

Tip #2. Make things easy for yourself. Certain situations might make you really uncomfortable, scared, or upset. This can be especially frustrating if this prevents you from doing things you want to do in peace. I always ask myself a few questions: Does this need to get done? Do I want to do it? If yes to either of the former, how can I do it in a way that won't spoil the rest of my day?

Problem:	**What I did:**
If I start googling news articles about sexual assault, I'll end up doing it for hours, feeling worse and worse as time drags on.	I pulled myself away and did some laundry instead. I focused on how the textures of different fabrics felt on my hands.
This movie has a pretty graphic scene, and I'm feeling sensitive today— if I watch it, I'll probably end up feeling spacey and numb.	I asked a friend to warn me when the scene would come up— when she did, I left to get some popcorn.
If I go out walking alone tonight, I'll be too nervous to have fun.	I still went out walking, but I brought my big scary dog along.

Tip #3. Are you angry? It's okay to be furious. It's also okay if you feel like forgiving, but you might instead want to hold a grudge for the rest of your life. That's A-OK. Being angry doesn't make you a bad person; whatever happened *should not have happened.* Period. It's okay to feel cheated about that! Know that you don't have to feel selfish for being mad, and that it's good to let yourself feel it, as long as you aren't hurting yourself or others. Here are some ways you can channel your anger into useful things:

- Do something physical. Swim, bike, kick-box, run, even kayak. If you have a sport of choice, play hard.
- Make a collage or draw a picture. Imagine that you are untouchably pure. Create something beautiful for yourself.
- When I feel overwhelmed with anger, I like to use that energy to clean my room. I'll toss everything from my desk drawers onto the floor and throw away what I don't need. There's something deeply satisfying about throwing old things into the trash.
- Feel the self-love in your anger. If you've spent too long explaining away wrongs, tucking your fury into hidden pockets and pretending it doesn't exist, feeling that rage can be both terrifying and beautiful. Ultimately, it shows that you've decided to take your own side.

Tip #4. Do you feel scared? I used to feel scared pretty much all of the time. It was exhausting. The best thing to do is to focus completely on the present. Look around you. Feel the ground under your feet. Feel the air in your lungs. Deep breath, in and out. Now say to yourself, *"In this precise moment, I am okay."*

Tip #5. Do you feel frozen or far away? There are tons of different things to do when you start feeling numb or frozen, like a ghost outside of your body.

- Counting colors is my personal go-to. I'll look at everything in my field of vision and count, say, only red things. *Shoes, jacket, stop sign, taillight, red, red, red.* Then I'll move on to green. Then blue. It's a way for me to engage my sense of sight without any pressure to think too hard.

- Make physical contact with something. Whether it's giving yourself a foot massage, having a cup of hot tea, receiving a hug from a trusted friend, or just feeling a fuzzy blanket, it can be grounding to focus on simple touches.
- Tell yourself the basics, over and over. For example: *"My name is Ruby Walker. I am sixteen years old. I am at school. I am wearing a blue jacket. My name is Ruby. I'm sixteen. I'm sitting by a tree in the courtyard. The bench is warm. I'm Ruby. I'm sixteen."*

Tip #6. Repeat after me:
I deserve to heal.
I deserve respect.
I deserve compassion.
I am not alone.

CHAPTER 6

Create something.

I can feel it when I'm not expressing myself. It feels like car
sickness: a dull ache in my head. My stomach starts to roil.
Thoughts repeat again and again— images enter my mind
and then hide away when I pay them any attention, like
dreams forgotten during breakfast. Do you ever get that
feeling? Like everything is happening to you while you float along,
changing nothing, becoming nothing? Do you ever get scared at
night?

A semester into my new college life, I had an existential crisis.
I think casual conversation has watered down those words. "Oh,
sorry," I hear people say, "I just had an existential crisis for a second there." But when I say it, I don't mean a few minutes of con-
fusion. I mean the original brand, the whole enchilada — crying,
despair, rage, relief, and terror. Someone took a pitchfork and
started churning the foundations of my worldview like ripe com-
post. It was like expecting another stair step and feeling that split-
second fall.

Who am I? What is my purpose? What does it all mean? If I am free, what actions are worth choosing? How could I impact anything? Why am I me, and not someone else?

But I was already dedicated to recovery. I wasn't going to let some existential dread stop me from living my life. So I started doing some research, and I discovered that I was not, in fact, the first person to ever *freak the living hell out* about what it means to be alive.

I come from a long tradition of very confused human beings. And so do you.

A smart Norwegian named Zapffe once offered a framework which might explain how we all get on, knowing what we know, without sitting around shaking with worry for hours every day. He said that folks tended to deal with the scary questions in life in a combination of four ways:

1. **Anchoring.** The fact that there really aren't any objective rules on how to be a living human is terrifying, so people tend to have something that they decide to believe in any-way. This could be a value like love, a religion, a country, a political ideology, the future, a moral philosophy, or even parenthood.
2. **Isolation.** This means straight up refusing to think about anything negative. It's pretty metal, but I usually can't pull it off.
3. **Distraction.** This just means getting so caught up in the physical world that there's no time to get introspective. "Screw thinking about death, I need to score 1500 on the SAT!" Or having lots of sex, if that's your cup of tea. Just... doing stuff without thinking.
4. **Sublimation.** This means directing that anxiety and using it to make something—art, writing, expression, under-standing. In chemistry, sublimation is when something goes directly from a solid to a gas. Ever seen dry ice? It looks like magic. Sublimation means transforming your fears from something *obstructive* into something *creative*.

Self-expression is a very down-to-earth and practical way to handle difficult thoughts and feelings. For me, writing is how thought becomes real. My pen scrapes against the page. I can touch it, feel it, burn it, destroy it, tack it up on my wall, share it, or keep it in a closed book for eternity and after. I can talk to myself. Oftentimes when I write in my journal, I'm not looking to write something that sounds good. I'm not looking to create art, or literary merit, or even be able to read my handwriting in two weeks. I just need to organize myself. I need to make my little handprint on the world.

Self-expression is something we need very deeply as human beings. It isn't a frivolous luxury. We've had art from the earliest traces of civilization; from the first time someone marked the inside of a cave with a handprint, looked at it and thought, "That is mine."

When I am alone and my fears push me into the tiniest piece of myself, art is how I shout back, "I will not be made small! I will not be silenced! This world is not all good, but I will *claw my piece of beauty from it*, and there is *nothing* you can do to stop me!"

It's a connection with the Earth. That might be where the impulse comes from. In every society, in every mind, whether the urge is satisfied or starved, people have a need to make some mark on the face of eternity. If you express yourself in any way, you've just created an irreplaceable and unique piece of the world; you've made the human experience just a little bit richer; you've eased your worried mind. And that's worth something.

> "The arts are not a way to make a living. They are a very human way of making life more bearable. Practicing an art, no matter how well or badly, is a way to make your soul grow, for heaven's sake."
> — Kurt Vonnegut, *A Man Without a Country*

ADVICE ON HOW TO STAND UP, FREAK OUT, AND REMAKE THE WORLD:

Tip #1. Be an amateur! Write a bad poem, draw an ugly picture, keep a journal written in scrawling shorthand. This self-reflection isn't work. It isn't for anybody but you. If you'd like to share, that's wonderful— but everybody needs an outlet, even when it isn't pretty. Sewing, paper crafts, coloring, singing, piano, painting, dance. The thoughts that keep you up at night don't need to die, they need *out*. Anything you can create is a step in the right direction.

Tip #1. Journal. Write a journal entry in any old book any scrap of paper, with anything, plainly. Don't say everything that's ever happened. You don't need to detail your whole day. Just write down something you noticed recently— What did you think of it? How did that make you feel?

Write another when you notice something striking again. It could be a day or a month later. Set time constraints if it suits you. I always found it difficult to keep a daily, comprehensive diary. It was always too much or too little.

Tip #2. Write a letter. Date it. "To myself in 2021" or some such. Decorate it if you'd like. I found one of my old letters recently and it made me very happy. I had met the goals my past self set for me.

Tip #3. More creative ways to cope.
- Photograph your favorite places in the neighborhood
- Draw a four-panel comic about a friend.
- Think of the outfit you could wear that would be the most "you." write about it.
- Press flowers under something heavy— choose your favorite.
- Write a song— bang on an instrument and sing anything

you like. If your life were a musical, what would you call today's number?

- Go outside. Breathe. Write about everything you see, feel, touch, and taste.
- Pick eight songs that remind you of someone or something you like. Make a playlist.
- Dance by yourself. Imagine you are under dazzling lights.
- Make a collage of magazine bits that remind you of a good memory.
- Pick something and list exactly 10 kinds of it.

CHAPTER 7

Failure is not the end.

So you've failed. You didn't get the job, the part, the date, the promotion; you quit the race; you lost the game. A knot closes around your throat. You tip your head back and decide the ceiling is very interesting because that's all you can do not to cry. When I was depressed, one minor cock-up had the power to take me down for days. It wasn't even the fact that I didn't get what I wanted that got me so down, no, it was the Tornado of Shame and Blame that I always fell ass-first into afterwards.

You may be familiar with this tornado. It starts innocent enough, with a teal sky and a few sharp gusts of wind whipping at your woolen frock. It starts with, "I forgot to turn in my Chemistry homework." Then the wind pushes harder, and you start to think, "I'm going to fail chemistry." In a few minutes you're really freaking out. It's gone from "I'll never get into a good college," to "I'm going to die poor and forsaken in a drainage ditch because I don't have the work ethic for steady employment!" By this time your feet are no longer touching the ground. Broken glass and slabs of sheetrock knock against your ragdoll body. Welcome to the cyclone!

This tornado is also called catastrophic thinking. It's basically when "One thing went wrong," takes a few half-logical steps and becomes, "Nothing will ever be right again, and it's all my fault!"

The thing is, everyone fails sometimes. That's why there's such an absolute glut of cliché advice on the issue. And everyone's got something deep and inspiring to say about how much failure has taught them, how grateful they are for the trials and tribulations, how screwing things up is actually a blessing!

All that might seem true when you're looking back from a better place, but what about when you're in the thick of it? Trying to force a veneer of joy onto a harrowing situation doesn't always do much good.

I'm not the kind of person who naturally feels grateful for messing things up. I still get angry about the mistakes I make. Learning to deal with failure better is a choice, not to suppress all negative emotions, but to focus my energy on something more productive than catastrophic thinking and self-hatred.

You can't choose how you feel, but you can choose what you do about it! And I've discovered that even minor failures like going to bed too late go much smoother when I do these four things:

Recognize that feeling disappointed is inevitable but temporary.

Oh gosh, I have to get up at 7AM and now it's 3:30. I'm really sad I didn't plan my evening better than this! I wanted to get enough rest to face the day. Well, there's nothing to do now.

Move on from the failure ASAP when it's over.

Well, I can't undo this mistake. All I can do is get to bed as soon as possible right now, because this present moment is all I can change. I'll go brush my teeth.

Figure out how to avoid a repeat performance.

Tomorrow I really ought to outline a bedtime routine. I know using my phone in bed effects my circadian rhythms. Maybe I should charge it in another room and dig up that old alarm clock, so I'm not tempted?

Find *something* to be positive about.

Things aren't so bad. I don't have anything to do tomorrow night, so if I'm sleepy all day I can crash as early as I want. All I have to do is get through the morning, and I already know I'm capable of that. Things are going to be alright.

See, if I had let myself think catastrophically, I probably would've said "screw it" and stayed up all through the night. I would've been too caught up in blame to look for solutions.

Failing hurts bad no matter how you swing it. When you try your hardest and fail, it feels like the best of you wasn't good enough; when you don't try your hardest, you feel like you're lazy. There's always that sting of regret: why didn't I give it a little more?

You don't have to revel in these feelings, nor do you need to be ashamed of them. Whether you've done right or wrong in the past, it doesn't matter. All you can affect now is your future. All you need to do is keep your head on straight. The future holds moments of joy you can't even imagine yet.

STORYTIME: THE SUMMER PASSING BY

In the dumb tween books I read, it went like this:

A girl walked through the cafeteria alone, holding tight to a plastic lunch tray.

She tripped over a boy; he grinned, apologized, took her hand, and said, "Are you okay?"

"Oh- Yeah," she stuttered, "You just have some... Spaghetti... On your shirt."

After that, something in the girl's chest grew warm when he called her Spaghetti Girl.

But I don't remember exactly how we met for the very first time. I know it started with a sixth-grade theater class.

"So, if you think about it," I rambled, "At this point? The ocean has to be at least twelve percent whale sperm. No thanks!"

I looked up from the doodles on my notebook to the tall girl standing by my desk. *Oh, no. Wait. That was weird!* I was still getting used to it, see—being weird. Fifth grade was sort of easier, even though it was my very first time in public school, since Horn elementary at least had a uniform. That had eliminated some tough decisions.

But even when I looked like everyone else, they could tell I wasn't the same on the inside. I'd gone to a series of free-roaming Austin hippie private schools as a little kid, where I learned acroyoga from Michael the P.E./art teacher, and we all made gluten-free soup on Wednesdays. I knew how to make friends at my old schools. At Dahlstrom Middle in rural Buda, Texas, though? It seemed like my classmates were all following some huge rule book they'd never sent me a copy of. I was trying to get it all straight in my head: talking about the differences between lagomorphs and rodents was weird; correcting the teacher's spelling was mostly fine, but correcting her when she said the civil war wasn't about slavery *wasn't;* raincoats were not supposed to be worn inside.

Even I could tell that mentioning *aquatic jizz* in class was cross-ing a line. I braced myself for the girl in front of me to pull away (smiling politely or grimacing, it all meant the same thing) and make an excuse to find another seat. Instead she just laughed with all her teeth out, said, "It's probably up to at least fifty now," and sat down in the next desk over. We whispered through class, little jokes about the teacher's wispy white hair or how often he brought up The Beatles. When the bell rang, I realized I'd forgotten to get her name. I caught my new friend by the door.

"What's your name?" I asked.

"Jasmine," said the girl.

She took my hand and shook it.

I asked Jasmine if she'd eat lunch with me, and soon we were stuck together every day. Turns out, we both had two parents, two brothers, a confused opinion on small dogs, and a passion for art. We both liked anime, emo music, cowboy boots, and barbie movies. We both felt separate from the Christian girls who wore big white bows in their hair and we didn't quite know why.

She called me on Skype when I got bronchitis again, and I couldn't come to school.

The calls went from careful appointments, asking, "Can I call you at six?" to "Surprise, loser!" very fast. Sometimes we watched movies or read manga; sometimes we drew; sometimes we talked for hours about nothing much at all. It was nice to have a friend.

In the movies I watched, it looked like this:

The girl's best friend had found a boy to kiss. The girl was happy for her; there was a shot of her over their shoulders, smiling warm and bright.

As it happened, it was so dark in Jasmine's room I could barely see her, the little skype video call grainy on my clunky old laptop. I could make out her green-rimmed glasses, her teeth fluorescent white against an even brown complexion.

"You have a *what?*"

"I have a boyfriend," she said again.

"How come you haven't mentioned him before?"

"I don't know."

"Do you like him a lot?"

She shrugged. "Not really."

"Then why are you two going out?"

I didn't know why, but this was making something flip in my stomach. Who was this guy? What was his name? What was his *deal?* Couldn't he tell she didn't really like him? Couldn't he tell he was light years away from deserving her time?

"He asked me to," she said, like it was that simple.

"You know," I said, "You don't have to say yes just because someone asks." When she broke up with him the next week, I didn't even try to feel bad. The feeling started in my chest but didn't stay there. It went all the way up to my face until I couldn't help but smile.

In the books I was still rereading, it happened like so:

"What? Are you going to say something?" The girl turned on the boy when he spoke, as fast as the crack of a whip. Rain fell around them, stinging cold, as the party raged on inside. He pulled her closer, his hand on her waist hot by contrast. She glared up into his endless charcoal eyes.

"I hate you," she said.

"No you don't," he said.

She closed her eyes and kissed him for the first time because that was easier than admitting he was right.

At that time, in real life, it meant nothing.

It's going down, I'm yellin' timber, you better move, you better dance!

We finished the song and laughed, hyped up on pop music and the chocolate cupcakes Mom had made for my 12th birthday party. The room was small, just a karaoke machine at the front and a table by the back, lit up in soft orange light that bounced the faux-bamboo walls and made everything glow. Jasmine and I piled into one side of the vinyl booth while Zoe and Caylee took the other.

"Hey," said Jasmine, "Have y'all heard of *the pocky game?*"

The others peppered her with questions like "What's that?" and "Do we need cards?"

I just shook my head. "Okay, so, basically you get a pocky, which is like a long piece of chocolate, and you pick your opponent," she said, turning to me. I put up my fists like we were going to fight. Her face scrunched up into a giggle. "Shut up, Ruby. Anyway, you each bite off one end of it, and whoever breaks off first, loses!"

"Loses what? Just loses?" Zoe sounded bored. Suddenly, for no reason at all, I wanted to fight her.

"Let's play! C'mon," I pleaded.

We all scrambled to find something pocky-like on the table, and eventually settled on one section of a Kit Kat bar. The instrumental to *Timber* was still playing on loop while Zoe and Caylee started their game.

Zoe broke almost immediately, and we laughed.

I realized too late that I'd overestimated the length of a kit kat. Jasmine's face was right on mine, so close I couldn't look without going cross-eyed. Closing my eyes would be even weirder. I took a bite of chocolate, small as can be, as Jasmine did the same. Wasn't she going to stop? We didn't have much left. I could feel her breath on my lip.

It was too much. I broke first, to our little audience's dismay.
"Awww!"

"Boo! You should've kissed!"

"Lame."

So I leaned over, put my hand on her shoulder, and kissed her. Just the barest thing, a peck on the lips, then gone. Zoe clapped a hand over her mouth, and they both went, "Oooooh."

I wouldn't look at Jasmine, though I could hear her startled laughing. I was too embarrassed, embarrassed to not be embarrassed, worried because I felt half-crazy— concerned because I didn't *care*. I laughed too, desperately, and for a moment everything was light and free. Jaz pulled me up and we sang *I Kissed A Girl*, letting the others in on our big joke.

In the fanfictions I was starting to read, it happened all at once, like this:

The boy's stomach dropped out from under him. He couldn't believe it. *I'm not gay*, he thought, *I can't be*. Did this mean he was in love with his best friend? The whole world swirled into a pinpoint of panic, chaos before the big bang, and then exploded. Nothing would ever be the same again.

"Look at me," his best friend said, bringing him back to Earth, "We're going to be okay." He covered his hand with his own, and held tight. Somehow, looking into his best friend's eyes, the trials they'd face in the world didn't seem so bad. They had *this simple feeling* between them—whatever it was.

My revelation was less of a transformation and more of a math problem finally making sense. *Oh, when I kissed her, I did like it*. I let that thought sit for a few weeks. Then I got on the computer and searched, "Am I gay quiz?"

When the results came in, I kept it to myself.

In the world of fiction, the little moments always meant something.

"I miss you," the boy said, like there was a bad taste in his mouth.

"And what am I supposed to do about that?" Said his best friend, going still.

"I don't know. What do you want to do?"

"I wanna stay."

In real life, we never talked about what was real. As we got closer and let our guards down, I read meaning into every breath; I couldn't find the lines to divide facts from lies and daydreams.

"My internet friend has a huge crush on me, and I wanna let her down easy," Jasmine blurted one day after school. "Is it okay if

I add you to the chat and say you're my boyfriend?"

"That's the dumbest thing I've ever heard," I said, "Of course I'm in."

We decided my fake name would be Will because my grandpa was named William. I ended up liking her friends a bit too much. Anna, Kelsie, and Rachel were from California; Maja was from Sweden; Abel was from France. We'd all send each other little drawings of bees or fish or flowers. We watched movies together and mocked them in the chat.

It was a game of secrets. Jasmine and I made things up about ourselves, and the fun was in keeping it all straight. I was five foot eleven. My middle name was Keaton. She had a pierced nose. I said we spent time together after school, which was a lie, but that her mom didn't like me, which was true. She called me "babe" sometimes, even when we were alone. I tried not to wonder how much of it was a joke.

Jasmine always fell asleep when we talked late into the night. I'd see her on the screen, cheek squished against her hand, glasses falling off.

"Jaz," I said softly.

She mumbled.

"Goodnight, Jaz."

I knew it was just the meds hitting, but I liked to think I helped too. Wouldn't it be nice if I made her feel safe? When we talked, Jasmine slept. She was an insomniac.

Jasmine was the only one at my thirteenth birthday, and that was fair enough, since I was the only one at hers. I wrapped my arms tight around her shoulders— she didn't seem quite stable enough to pick me up like this, but I trusted her. "Hey, hey, hey!"

She said, "I'm not gonna drop you, dumbass." The grass lurched towards me when she leaned forward, snickering.

"You're a maniac!" I yelped.

"You love me."

"I can't wait for you to die."

In all the stories I read, it stopped. One way or another, through resolution or just by fading away, the emotions reached a conclusion. It went like this:

"I love you," he said.

"I love you too," she said.

In my life, it only got worse— the doubt, the elation. Twelve, thirteen, fourteen. I didn't have the courage to say something and ruin our friendship, but I wasn't strong enough to be a real friend, either. I was a double agent. I hated myself. I knew I'd never hurt her on purpose, but when it rained outside and she pressed her cold feet to my calf and her laughing face to the back of my neck, I couldn't ignore the feeling that I had malicious intent.

In the books I read, the turning point made sense. It was some big incident, and it went like this:

"You need to stop lying to me," she said.

"I don't think I know how," he said.

When I was fifteen and just starting community college, I reached my limit quietly. We sat on the steps in front of an empty glass-fronted building, the sounds of a small carnival a few yards away. *Dieciséis de Septiembre*— Mexican independence. "I wish we could go inside," Jaz said, her eyes cutting toward the dead, locked doorway, "I remember coming here a lot as a kid."

"Do your parents still go?"

"No, no, they're not that devout. It was mostly for holidays, when the church would throw big parties. My nana is serious about it, though. She's ninety, and she was still baking cakes for this thing until last year. Did you meet her?"

I laughed, "Yeah, after that last Halloween. She kept trying to giving us more candy."

"Oh, the horror. More candy."

I kicked her ankle. "I didn't have enough room in my basket, you heinous witch!"

"I still wish I could've shown you inside." She pivoted with a sad smile, ignoring me while she looked right at my face.

I could never tell how much of her levelheadedness was for show. I was constantly freaking out and getting my gross feelings all over her, and she acted like she honestly didn't notice. How much of that was an act? How much of any of this was real? I couldn't take it anymore.

I examined our shadows on the ground below the steps, joined at the hip; if I didn't look away right then, I would've done something stupid like try to kiss her.

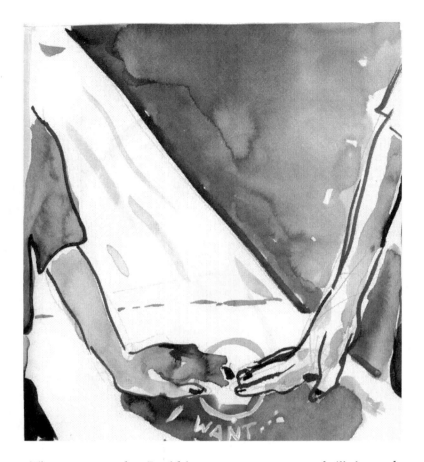

The very next day, I told her over text, a coward till the end.
I waited.

"No answer *is* an answer," I told myself, but part of me was still waiting on that juvenile hope— "I'm obsessed with you too." An affirmation, a confession. Anything to align my fantasies of how this was *supposed to go* with reality.

The longer I heard nothing from her, the more unlikely that outcome seemed.

I put all the things that reminded me of her into a bag. A string of carnival tickets, a little stuffed bear, and a shirt I had borrowed years ago. I tucked it in the highest place in my closet. No answer was an answer, but this thing we were doing? Where we didn't talk about it? That was killing me.

I just wanted my best friend back.

In the movies, they're never better off as friends. It never goes like this:

"Hey, you're right next to his dick!"

"Oh, come on, don't!" She covered her face with her hands while I snapped a photo.

We probably didn't have to whisper, but something about the Blanton Museum of Art's statue gallery demanded some modicum of respect. She grabbed for her phone and took a picture of me in retaliation. A marble replica of some old Greek statue stood between us, *au naturale*.

What was it the Greeks said about love? Weren't there different kinds?

What I felt then wasn't less than what I'd been feeling for all those years before. It was just... different. *Eros* turned to *philia*, and it wasn't just okay, it was better. Our friendship was honest in a way it never had been, a confusing game of secrets giving way to something strong that might've been there all along, if I'd only looked past my expectations.

I turned and went into the second room of statues, and I didn't have to look back to know she was with me.

"And autumn comes when you're not yet done
With the summer passing by."
—Mitski

ADVICE ON HOW TO ACKNOWLEDGE FAILURE, FIND SOLACE, AND MOVE ON:

Tip #1. Recognize the process. You've heard this a million times. Failure is normal, natural, and good. So is eating your placenta. But for some reason, they both just don't *feel* right.

Well I'm here to tell you, honestly, I hate failing! And I hate cheesy advice about getting on horses and all that other hogwash!

You don't need to enjoy failure, but here's the tough news: you kind of don't have a choice as to whether or not you experience it. We're constantly failing at something— may as well make the slightest attempt to have fun with it.

Tip #2. Draw yourself failing at something. Done? Now flip to the next page.

Draw balloons around yourself. And confetti. And a party hat. *Welcome to being alive.*

Tip #3. Make a bad-day backup plan. Sometimes you try something, and not only does it not work, it turns into a too-hot car full of steaming, rotten misfortune and ruins your entire day/week/life.

Here's my own checklist for un-ruining a day.

- Breathe deep. Say to yourself, "The past has passed. I only have power over my future. I have time." Really, why should you only get a fresh start once a day? What power does the stupid sunrise have over you? Time is fake. Every single moment is a chance to improve. You set the rules.
- Are you physically uncomfortable? Take care of that first. Take an Advil, eat some crackers, brush your teeth.
- Pick something small to do. Like making your bed or polishing your shoes. Imagine yourself doing it. Hear how it'll sound when your sheets slip against each other.
- Do it.
- You're on a roll already! Drink a glass of water.

- Do something creative. Compose a haiku, draw a cat, dance, sing. A day used to create— however small the creation— is never wasted. You just added to the universe.
- Do something physical. A short walk is fine. A bike ride is better. This is how I kickstart myself.

Tip #4. Update your failing vocabulary. Tired of wallowing? When something goes to crap, the best thing to do is move by fast. You can ride a bike over big potholes if you have enough momentum. Don't lose momentum!

WHAT TO SAY INSTEAD OF "I SUCK":
- I'll get it next time.
- I'm disappointed, but not defeated.
- This is how we learn!
- I wish _____ had gone better, but I'm okay.
- Experiencing failure doesn't make me a failure.
- Life goes on. I go on.
- I control my reactions, not my circumstances.
- Having a bad experience doesn't make me bad.
- Life is a mixed bag!
- I can overcome this.
- I will overcome this.

CHAPTER 8

What's really going on?

Y ou might notice that the feelings shown to the right are not following any known laws of fluid mechanics. That's the magic about repressing emotion; you put it away in your pocket, and it comes out of your hair. It doesn't make sense. Refusing to properly process a heartbreak could give you

feelings - fig. A

an anxiety attack about bees. Stress over school has given me stress about ear infections; grief over my uncle's death has sent me into a panic over an art class assignment.

Essentially, it's a whole lot of trouble. The best way to deal with problems is radically; meaning *from the source, from the root.* When you discover the source of your stress, you can understand why you're feeling the way you do and deal with it in a productive way.

Recently I lost a pair of headphones, which I needed to listen to music while running. I was furious. I knew for a fact they had been right there on the floor, but they weren't anymore. The pockets of all my jeans turned out empty. I had to hurry; there was only so much daylight left. I checked every corner of the house, pacing, growing increasingly frustrated— which only served to annoy my older brother Chance. He found me on the back deck, leaning on the wide red rail.

"Here, I have a pair," he snapped, shoving them into my fist. "Just take these and go running! All you're doing is stomping around and screaming, and it's starting to piss me off."

"It's not—" I worked my hands through my hair, pulling, pulling, "I'm just going out of my mind because they were *right there* and my room is *perfectly clean!* I saw them yesterday when I was cleaning! Alicia was with me!"

"You know what, if you don't want those then I'm gonna take them and go skating. You're acting like a brat."

"Shut up."

"I'm trying really hard to make you happy. Can you just stop?"

I did stop; everything stopped. I could still feel the anger in my body, but I no longer claimed it. "You're right. I'm overreacting, I know I'm overreacting. I'm just—" I took a deep breath and went out like a popped balloon, "I'm not doing okay."

Dry lightning licked up the edge of the horizon, thunderless. It wasn't about the stupid headphones. The week before, Chance and I had been out skateboarding near a neighborhood school when we saw the wreckage of an expensive vandalism. Flooding, broken windows, and what we thought was smoke from a fire. We called the police.

They kept us up all night and asked questions in the morning— why were we there? What were we doing? Are you sure you didn't go into the library? I told them everything I knew. Lies, lies, lies, they said. I knew it was a tactic, but it still worked like a charm.

"I'm— I'm trying, I'm trying so hard to remember what I think you want me to but I just can't." I sobbed.

Good Cop said, "It's okay."

Bad Cop said, "Now it's funny, because I never have this much trouble remembering things that happened six hours ago. Will you tell me why your story keeps changing?" The charges dropped like we knew they would when the video evidence came in, but the fact that I was no longer in danger of jail time didn't make me any less shaken.

It felt stupid once I realized what was going on. I was tossing up a fit about a misplaced item because I felt like I didn't have any control over my world, myself, or my memory.

Everyone gets caught up in distractions: those problems that seem like a big deal but are only a concern because it's easier to face a phantom; it's less psychologically uncomfortable to confront an issue that has no real weight in the first place. But this also means a distraction will never truly be solved. Real problems have real solutions, but distractions just distract. The only way to finally be free from a distraction is to find its cause.

STORYTIME: IN UGLIER WAYS

I was not thrilled with adolescence. It felt like I was turning into a monster, and nobody noticed but me. Or maybe everyone noticed. Everyone saw, and nobody had any shred of sympathy for the fact that I was experiencing a horrific transformation. It was exactly like that scene from The Mummy which gave me nightmares as a child, the one where the scarab beetle got under a man's skin and started crawling.

When I was ten, a lump the size of a nickel developed under my left nipple. I could feel it, just slightly move it around with my fingers. It was painful and tender when pressed. Just as I grew concerned about the asymmetry, another appeared on the right side. The internet told me they were called "breast buds," but to me they did not feel like flowers. They stuck out of my clothing, pointy and unnatural. I knew it was normal, objectively, but it felt very wrong. I was a regular kid, reading Percy Jackson and climbing the big Magnolia tree in my yard.

Then— things started existing on my body that weren't there before. How could that be right?

My only comfort was that one day would be shaped like a
woman, which I assumed boys would readily approve of. I really
can't recall thinking of my developing body in terms of *my* preferences, *my* feelings, how *I'd* like to look. I always thought of boys.
When I grew tall, I thought of whether a tall girl could still be
desired. When I found my female anatomy, I crammed a few fingers inside, trying to imagine how I'd accommodate. When the hair
under my arms grew thick and dark, I shaved it off, and my legs
too, and between them—

I looked at myself and I imagined others' looking at me.

Which is to say, I don't think I had a particularly bad childhood. I was loved and respected by my family and friends. But in the world, I saw magazines and movies where made-up starlets glistened flawlessly, and I saw pornography where girls were tugged around by the scalp and claimed to like it. I saw women who didn't look like any natural human looked, and because I didn't look that way, I thought, "Wow, I must be a monster."

I had to say all this because it's context. I hated the things that grew out of my body, my breasts, my hair—even as I imagined they could someday make me sexy. That's what I wanted to be: sexy, not comfortable; pretty, not able; wanted, not admired. So I already felt a mounting sense of horror towards every piece of my warping, traitorous skin. Acne was just the last straw. Something bad at the core of me was leaking out, one pimple at a time. That had to be why I was ugly.

I did theater in high school, and there it was natural for me to compare myself to the other girls. Freshman year I understudied for Jessie Macmillan in our one-act production of The Glass Menagerie. This meant that my principal job after school from four to six PM was to watch Jessie's every move, so I could learn her (our) blocking. But sometimes I forgot about that.

Our theater was small and dark, a rubbery black stage set six inches above the ground. Bats lived in the attic; it smelled like guano some days, after rain. Jessie sat on a wooden bench under warm yellow lights.

She played an old woman, but she was fifteen, and she looked it. She was tallish and quite thin, with pretty pixie features and long blonde hair. I watched her fuss and yell, affecting the accent of an old southern belle. The stage was harsh on contrast, and I could see that her skin was perfectly smooth—nothing like mine, marred with pustules and scabs that seemed to eat up more of my face every day.

She stood and moved stage left, scolding the senior who played Tom. I skimmed my fingertips over my forehead unconsciously. Bumpbumpbumpbumpbumpbumpbump. It was a shameful topography. I shouldn't have been so angry, but what did she do to deserve to be perfect? I scratched a little bump off from above my eyebrow, felt again, and it still wasn't smooth. What piece of myself would I have to remove to get those bumps to go away? I didn't care what. I'd do it. I just wanted them gone.

When I got home that night, and many nights after that, I got rid of what I could.

I leaned over my bathroom sink and squeezed little white worms out of my nose, my chin, my cheeks. I knew I shouldn't be doing it, but I'd hone in on one thing— one little blackhead, a huge gaping hole filled with toxic sludge. One night there was one above my lip, just to the left of my cupid's bow— a beady black eye, daring me from the rotten depths of my flesh. I squeezed. Its neighbors fled my skin. Sebum from pores adjacent squirmed out; I wiped it from my fingertips unsatisfied.

Something very deep inside me recognized that spot of oxidized oil as a foreign object invading my body, and I wanted it out. It's the same part of your brain that activates when you have to chew your arm off to escape the rubble of an earthquake: the small, scared, desperate part of you that'll do anything it takes to be safe. I ignored the sting.

My fingernails marked me with furious red crescents, but that *thing* stayed put. I changed angles and pressed again. And so what if I was overreacting?

A piece of the blackhead came out. I scratched it off, breaking skin, and pushed harder. I changed angles and pushed again. It was easier to look at wounds than foreign bodies in my skin.

On some days, if I woke up very early in the morning, I could sneak up on the monster when she was still just a girl. If I rose and splashed my face just as the day's first light shone butter yellow through my bathroom window, the part of me that held so much disgust sometimes refused to load. As if something that was always there came into focus, I saw my face as a face again, instead of a minefield. I looked like a woman. I looked clean.

I remember one of these mornings very clearly— it was my first morning back from that spring break camping trip, just a month after I dropped out. I hadn't washed my face or looked at myself, really, in four days. My hair was thick and sticky with lake-water, and I ached in that all-over sort of way that you ache after you've had an excellent time.

My room was exactly like I left it. Clothes covered the bed and lay on the floor as remnants of my packing frenzy. I threw my backpack down and headed for the bathroom.

I was expecting to look how I usually saw myself, as I was sure nothing major could've changed about my face in a few days, but that wasn't what I saw.

I didn't look how I thought I looked, which was usually puss-ridden and gangly. To my surprise, I looked how I felt. I was a piece of driftwood, washed up and waterworn, yet smooth from travel. All the things I usually hated were still there, but I didn't look like a monster anymore. For some odd reason, my eyes didn't immediately go to the spot on my cheek or the rude angle of my shoulders.

I took myself in as a whole: a form filled with life. A face with eyes to see and lips to taste and breathe. On my cheeks I saw freckles, little marks untainted by an anxious fixation with disease.

For once in a very long while, I did not see myself as a monster or a doll. I was a piece of nature whose form was suited to function and touched by experience, yet never disfigured. But this golden impression would sink back like the afterimage of a bright light soon enough. Nothing I did could make it last.

I broke my body into tiny pieces— are my lips too small? Is my nose too big? Are my legs too short? By attacking every piece I made sure I would never see myself whole. Divide and conquer.

I didn't realize how much energy it took to sustain a hatred like that until I could finally let it go. Like so many people, I walked around with a weight I didn't know I was carrying— always checking in windows, saucepans, and sunglasses to see if I was still inhuman.

I was tired of hating myself. I'd tried makeup and haircuts and push-up bras and more— was it all hopeless? Throughout my time alone, in befriending myself, in recovery, I wondered, is it possible that nothing I do will make me feel pretty? If it wasn't my skin it was my hair, and if it wasn't my hair it was my teeth, my figure, my asymmetrical face, my funny pigeon toes. I had to really ask myself, when was the last time I felt okay about my body?

And the answer ran right through me. I felt okay when I was *doing*. When I banged up my shins riding the flow of the San Marcos River, I wasn't thinking of how I looked. When my friend John and I danced on the roof of my tool shed, precariously, the milky way spilled out above us, I wasn't worried about moving with grace. When I woke up in the middle of the night and slipped out of my sandy sleeping bag on South Padre Island to find a good lump of bioluminescent seaweed to kick to life, I wasn't thinking of my tee shirt tan.

Did I obsess over my looks because I'm vain and materialistic? I don't think so. I think everyone grows up with a consuming desire to be valuable, lovable, and happy. The culture I was raised in told me I had to be flawlessly beautiful to be happy. But that was never true; the more I anguished over an ideal I'd never be able to reach, the more distracted I was from the things that actually made me feel good.

Reveling in the sensory experiences I find in nature.
Being a persistently loyal friend and being loved in return.
Creating art to match my vivid imaginings.
Speaking up for what I believe in, even when it's terrifying.
Moving my body and finding that I'm stronger than before.

Realizing what I'd misconceived about my looks wasn't the end of the monster. When I fixed my self-esteem, it wasn't like I realized I'd been beautiful all along and that solved my issues. I still had my days. I just stopped letting "I feel ugly" mean "I'm not worthy of respect."

Later in the fall when we'd all put our pumpkin decor out, I was so keyed up I could barely sleep. I had a Russian midterm in a few days. I drilled myself constantly:

Wife is zhena. *When a man is married, he's* zhenat. *Husband is* muzh. *When a woman is married, she's* zamuzhem. *What if she's married to a woman? No, you idiot, this is Russia, they don't allow that.*

And so on.

I caught myself in front of the mirror, tilting my head side to side, eyes combing my skin for spots and imperfections; it wasn't enough to notice the obvious things. I pulled my nose to the side and inspected the crook between nostril and cheek. I found I had a blackhead on my earlobe. There were tiny bumps at the corners of my lips.

I focused on a swollen little bump to the left of my septum, and I started pushing, pushing, itching to see some vile thing expel itself.

A muffled thought interrupted me then, like music you can feel from the next room over. *Is this wrong? Should I be doing this? Am I hurting myself?*

So I stepped back. I kept my eye on the mangled monster in the mirror. She stood to full height before me, a beast of keloid scars and jutting, wrong angles. I regarded her; I let her display her hairy hackles and slick yellow fangs.

"I think I'll leave you alone tonight," I said. Her terrible jowls spread in a brazen grin. We winked at each other.

Then I, the monster, left that bathroom. I had a test to ace.

"Unexpressed emotions will never die. They are buried alive and will come forth later in uglier ways."
— Sigmund Freud

ADVICE ON HOW TO SLAY THE HYDRA, OVERCOME YOUR DISTRACTIONS, AND FIND WHAT YOU TRULY FEEL:

Tip #1. Name your emotions.

It's okay to stop and say, "I'm feeling ____." For example: the other day I had a minor spat with my friend Jace. She said something that really hurt my feelings, but I didn't say anything back. Then, later in the night, I was having a tough time focusing on writing. I felt restless and I had no appetite. "You know what," I said, "I think I'm still angry about today. That actually hurt. I said it was fine, but it isn't. I'm pissed off." So instead of continuing to halfheartedly work on my book, I crawled into bed and wrote about the day I'd had. I detailed exactly why Jace was pissing me off so much. When I woke up the next day, I was still mad, but I felt less trapped.

You might notice patterns in the ways you repress certain things. For example, I get really anxious that I use the internet too much, when really, I'm just not getting enough sleep and that's why I'm having trouble focusing.

Tip #2. Redirect, redirect, redirect! For example, every time you start picking at your skin, make it a point to go watch your favorite guilty pleasure TV drama instead. Focus on something that makes you feel good. It's a lot easier to direct yourself into doing something positive than it is to *stop* yourself from doing something negative.

Tip #3. Come up with replacement habits.

- Get a piece of paper and make a list of things you know you do when you're stressed. Think back to an exam, a hard week, or a deadline.

- Are any of these things more destructive than helpful? Keep an eye out for distractions like: nitpicking, cutting, drinking or drug use, starting arguments, romantic pining, putting yourself down, obsessing over a celebrity, and worrying over yet-unforeseeable future events. Underline them. It's hard to stop a habit, especially a stress habit, but you can do it if you start small.

- List some healthier unstressers. Sometimes taking care of yourself means a warm bath while it's cold outside. Sometimes it's getting endorphins from a jog. Sometimes it means just facing that big paper head on. Nerves don't always mean you shouldn't do something -- sometimes they're just an indication that you feel this thing is important.

Tip #4. Analyze your behavior and plan for future distractions.

When are the times you feel most distracted, and why? When are the times you find it hardest to keep still? What are you avoiding? Are there clear trends in your behavior? For example, maybe when you're worried about a big competition coming up, you start obsessing over your weight?

If this is true, you can consciously say to yourself, "That tournament is in a week and I'm gonna be feeling really stressed out. I need to remember not to take my stress out on my body. I do this every time and it never helps! If I start getting worried about the way I look, I'll take a nice hot bath instead." Planning like this can really help mitigate unnecessary, distracting angst.

Tip #5. Learn what is really important to you.

Stopping yourself in the moment is a wonderful way to mitigate bad distractions— but if you can get deeper, that's better. You might get to a place where you *know* you only pick at your freckles when something else is on your mind, and so you can really just stop fussing over them.

We are all changing all the time. Notice your reactions, your feelings, and their causes. Journaling can really help with this. By knowing yourselves, we can be better equipped to guide the ways we are changing.

CHAPTER 9

Be yourself!

I had a personality beyond my depression. I had a world of quirks, tendencies, and beautiful unique truths about myself to discover. Mind clouded with sadness and hatred, I didn't always believe this. Wasn't I just a natural pessimist? It may feel like your mental illness (and all the habits and preferences that make up its body) is *the bulk of your personality*.

Not so! Not so!

I have become so much since I recovered from depression. Old things came back— how loud I am when I can find my voice, my love of birds, my love of art. Others are new:

I write now. I'm involved in local politics. I like to make people I don't know very well feel welcome at parties. I'm obsessed with cacti.

Knowing yourself is useful two ways. First off, any decision you make for yourself, whether it's to move to a new city or just be more comfortable in your skin, will work better if it's informed by your personal, unique attributes. Do you love to sleep in? Do you care a lot about children? Knowledge of who you are affects what you do, what will make you happy, and your success.

Second, having a positive idea of your identity is *nice on its own.* Not because it's advantageous, but because it's *right.* Living just feels better when you are surrounded by people who are affirming to your true, honest self. I have personal experience with this as a member of the LGBT community: realizing that there are aspects of you that are difficult to face in the first place is a necessary step towards self-acceptance and self-love.

Maybe you're the only Indian kid in your grade, you have a disability, your friends don't share your religion, you're transgender, you talk too fast, or you prefer not to talk much at all. Everyone has something about them that makes them different from others. You might not want to recognize that. You might want it to go away. That's *okay.*

I've had times when I've sincerely wished I could be a heterosexual. Right after I came out as a lesbian, not a bisexual, I noticed my guy friends treating me differently. They weren't as nice as they used to be. They paid more attention to girls they saw as sexually available, and I knew it was unconscious, but it still hurt. Was that all our friendship was worth? I couldn't change who I was, but I still ran in loops around it, wishing I could be normal.

But what's the *point* of trying to be "normal"? Really, what is it? Is anyone perfectly normal? And who sets the standard? I can't think of a more boring aspiration. If someone hates me for something I can't change, they just aren't my audience. I will never dull myself trying to be "normal" for them. I'll carefully choose the people whose opinions I really care about, and for them I will be *fantastic.*

WHAT I LEARNED ABOUT INSECURITIES FROM BEING GAY:
1. I will never get 100% of people to like me.

2. People are going to dislike me for parts of myself I just can't change.
3. I can't let my difference be my weak point.
4. If I face shame with pride, nobody can hurt me.

When all is said and done, I'm the only person on this Earth who will be present in my life every moment until my very last breath. Knowing myself deeply helps me connect to that life: through my relationships, my values, and through the face I choose to show the world. And the more I know, the more I can be sure that face is true.

STORYTIME: NOT YET FOUND.

I tried being a ghost.

I was stranded in a wilderness, with no clue who I was or where I was. It wasn't even that I was dissatisfied with my identity: I had *nothing*.

Every one of my identifying characteristics had been sand-blasted off of me. There was nothing to replace them. I loved disco, birds and science (before the depression.) I was an actor and a theater kid (before I dropped out of school.) I (used to) read books. I (used to) wear lots of aquamarine. I (used to) have straw-berry blonde hair.

I (used to) never see my dad.

I (used to) overachieve.

I (used to) talk too much.

I (used to) be fierce.

I was sharp, before— always ready with a retort, writing pam-phlets and petitions, letting it make my blood boil until I was brim-stone against the world and willing to prove it with sources MLA cited. In 6th grade, my science substitute insisted that mass was the same as weight, and I wrote her a paper on the difference, crafted from Times New Roman and spite. In 9th grade, I understudied for the role of Amanda Wingfield in the Glass Menagerie. I was off book a month early, though I only performed once. I was *an-noyingly* passionate.

Pressure and migraines, pressure and tears. I left Hays High a few days before my 15th birthday, and since then, I had nothing to do but waste my time. My friends joked that I was dead. "R.I.P. Ruby." I felt like a ghost, then. No face, no voice, unfinished busi-ness, just lingering.

I tried being a wunderkind. For a month I really expected my depression to leave my body as I left Hays. I planned every day for rigorous homeschooling. Electrical engineering, one hour. Then I'll read about Nikola Tesla. Then I'll write an essay on Robert Smalls. *If I work hard enough, I can't be lonely.*

I tried being odd.

I was talking to Dad again— he was a renegade, and he made me feel like one, too. We made benches out of recycled wood and positioned them around Texas State University. We listened to Buddy Holly and U2. I watched him build skateboards out of old water skis and charm strangers with the same four asinine jokes that always still worked on me.

Dad was a mashup of too many things: an absentminded professor, a skater punk, and a Texarkana Cowboy all at once. He was the kind of person who always messed up, but never made you hate him. A father you could rent for two nights on DVD but never keep — just a little too Dostoevsky and not enough responsible adult caretaker.

That was fine for me; I didn't want care. I wanted to wear a bandana with stolen glasses, talk to every stranger, and fray mint flavored picks between my teeth.

When I dropped out of high school, I leaned into that feeling of insouciant rebellion. My friend Holly sat me down on her bed-

room floor and dyed my hair bright red with no gloves. When she was done her hands looked like a curse.

I took a road trip into west Texas with my father, his 1994 Volvo destroying two tires over four hundred miles on a broken shock absorber. We went during finals week, and since my brother couldn't come, I felt doubly chosen. (Describing everything wrong with that car would fill the rest of this chapter.)

I tried being cool.

We almost didn't make it before dark, wood jammed into the Volvo's undercarriage keeping it all together for those last twenty miles.

"Wanna take a dunk in that reservoir up there?" Dad said.

"Just lemme get my shoes off," I said.

We dragged our machine's metal carcass from one end of 432 to another, wondering about how it'd feel to be born in a town like that in the desert, guts uncomfortably greased in convenience store chicken, buzzing from the days' hitchhike.

"Was he on meth?" I said.

"Probably," He said, "I'm just glad we got the new tire."

All the trappings of a fine road trip.

133

We pulled up to the Hotel Paisano, all dust and utterly hungry. It was the only place to stay in town that mattered. We ascended to the upper balcony, where I met ten or twenty people whose faces and names I'd forget in favor of testing how many hors d'oeuvres it was polite to consume immediately upon arrival. I was regaled with my dad's origin story — how he entered the film society on gumption alone at nineteen.

"His parents kicked him out," the forgettable guy said.

"No, no, see," My dad cut in, "My *divorced parents* just got to-gether and asked me, 'What are you doing with your life?'"

"Yeah, ouch, that spells trouble," I said.

"And I didn't have a clue! But I watched a lot of old movies. I said, 'Well, I'm gonna go to Austin and go to film school,' and I thought I had 'em there. But my mother got this sweet southern look on her face, and she said— 'Oh, that's just perfect. Your cousin is driving down to Austin tonight, why don't you go get in the truck with him?'"

I laughed and tried to be funny. Dad got me a tonic water from the bar. "Isn't a topo chico, but it'll do," he said.

I felt like I needed something stronger than water.

Could I do that? Could I be a master of making stuff up? I didn't have any gumption. Definitely not enough to float into the clouds like that, not enough to not care in the really cool way, where you legitimately don't worry, instead of the way I didn't care by caring a lot about disappearing completely.

This place looked like a fruit crate label— the old kind, hand painted, nothing but cyan, tan, and rich azure. There would be mountains in the distance and a cowboy up front, smile brighter than the inevitable full moon glimmering above him.

It was the specificity that really got to me. By the time they're six, every consumer of American media comes to understand a certain set of myths about the Wild West. We grow up. By 12, I understood that Cowboys vs Indians was a tragedy, not a game, and that the mythos of an old west of boundless free land and opportunity was predicated on theft and genocide.

Still, if some alien probe lifted the impression of "West" straight from my 8-year-old brain, based entirely in Woody action figures and the way Dad spoke of his stetson felt hat, and used that as the blueprint for a brand new software-generated place, that place would be Marfa, Texas.

My legs hung off the edge of the movie theater's concrete slab porch. Next to me, an old tan barbershop. Blue neon. Scrubby plains yawned up to kiss a marbled paper sky. I'd caught myself falling asleep to an art film and stepped outside to breathe. It was a two-hour visual essay on Los Angeles, and it was beautiful, but I didn't long for L.A. We have all the desert you could ever want right here in Texas, and better pools, to boot.

L.A. wouldn't fix me anyway. Its magic was a hat trick. How could anyone get to be *really* cool there? The kind where you aren't viewing yourself as a product whose sole value is congeniality?

Right here, I thought, filling the scuffs on my boots with sharpie, *here's all the desert I can take.*

The film makers party was uncomfortable in every way. It was all drunk snobs packed into a closed artisanal coffee shop, flashing lights pounding my ears in.

Dad was too fiftyish and considerate to get tipsy. I was too fifteen to react when a twentyish told me he *really* loved redheads. My sixteen texts to Jasmine weren't sending. But Prince had just died, so the musical tribute was excellent.

Dad unwrapped the projector. Eight millimeters and fully functional, with sample tape I'd scrapped together myself in our hotel room. The table at the front of the room was big enough for it, and I watched Dad explain the mechanism to a few enthusiastic young movie nerds.

I always thought of him as effortlessly charming. For some reason, tonight I could feel the effort. I felt interest in our project dwindle as it took more and more to get the projector working: *plug this in here, we'll go outside so it's dark, darn it, why's the picture upside down?* The harder we tried to make everything go well, the more I felt it was time to cut my losses and hide.

We got it running. A picture purred to life on the wall.

What do I always say about my jokes?" He said.
"Not funny," I said, leaving the bit unfinished.
I wasn't a prop in his routine.
"...But they're always timely."

We left the party on an exhale. It was hard to believe how hot it was just that morning. We swaddled the old projector and played TETRIS with it in the back seat of the Volvo.

Dad drove me out to see the lights. The car grew colder and colder as we exited the Earth's atmosphere and greeted the plains-grasses that dot the edge of low orbit. I expected to encounter alien life at any moment; I found that we were quite alone.

I decided, quite firmly, to never call my coach's jacket a wind-breaker again. The wind was blowing right through me. We stopped when the city was pocket size. I shivered and sat on the hood.

The thing is, I didn't need to look up to see them. Stars like you wouldn't believe. Lights that I can't explain any better than the first to do it— I made a noise and hugged Dad tight. "They look like pinholes. Like the Greeks or whoever said. Breaking into heaven."

He used his left to secure his hat against a gust, and I clasped his right hand.

Looking at the night sky and feeling small is only a cliche if you can say that getting burned by a fire is cliche. It's a timeless human truth.

I kept thinking of pinholes. I imagined a girl my age biting back curses at the magnitude of all she couldn't touch, and her bones buried here two thousand years ago. There is no "cool" when you turn to bone dust. All I'll have then is the love I gave and the stars I watched. I'll be buried with a hundred thousand things only I can remember.

I tried to get better.

I started school at Austin Community College. I started handling my breakdowns. My friend Evan told me again and again, "Ruby, you sound like a self-help book."

That made me cry. Turns out, being mentally healthy turns you into a cliché.

And I know I'd rather be happy and bland than tortured and interesting. Yet, sometimes it still makes me angry, that I don't have the option to destroy myself anymore.

Even though I don't want to! The loss of freedom is infuriating. And I feel lonely, being *good* all the time. The sort of person who goes jogging for fun. Too smart to return to a past I never wanted. Even if I did start drinking again, I could never force myself back into thinking it wouldn't kill me. I'm too aware of the consequences to even briefly enjoy the fall.

I'm trying to be a light.

I can't do everything perfectly. But I am good for good. Most of the time I can feel this energy shaking my lymph nodes. I know who I am: loved, empathetic, excitable, forgiving. I want to write the stories I needed before. I'm trying to be the friend I needed when I felt completely alone. I'm glad, somehow, that I felt all those terrible things and stumbled my way out. Only for having been there do I know where my little world needs light.

Being a light means being kind when it isn't required, good when nobody can see, and refusing to accept suffering as the status quo. I'm nothing like I was before: I let the things I care about take hold of my whole body.

Yet sometimes, when I get sad, I feel like I'm there again, a scared fourteen-year-old who can't tell anyone she's depressed.

I have my days.

I have my doubts.

I have some moments when I feel so sure of everything— Of my purpose, what I'm doing, who I am and how I feel. And I have days when it feels like I'm drifting out of it, or worse, drifting into something terrible. I start to avoid thinking about it.

What do I believe in? What am I trying to do? What does my future look like? Do I still believe in the things I used to?

I get so scared. I have to be reminded: these doubts are part of knowing myself. I am not drifting away, and I am not drifting into anything bad. Every human being feels lost sometimes. All that's required to fix it is some thought.

> "People often say that this person or that person has not yet found himself.
> But the self is not something that one finds. It is something that one creates."
> —Thomas Szasz.

ADVICE ON HOW TO GIVE IN TO DOUBT, CREATE YOURSELF, AND NEVER BE THE SAME:

Tip #1. Think about the little things.

- If you were in a library, all day, a huge library with nothing but time… what would you do?
- List some things that seem fun, but really aren't.
- What do you avoid doing, but enjoy once you're already doing it?
- What did you do for fun as a kid?
- Are you a bottle or a tap? Do you tend to suppress thoughts you don't like, or express them? I was always a tap. I'd lash out or break down. I have friends who always hold it all in— sometimes we're mixtures of both. How do you think you can find balance?
- How quickly do you adjust to changes? When someone gets a haircut, do you remember what they looked like before?
- Name 5 things that matter more than money.
- Name someone with a great personality. What do you admire about them? Is there any small way you can follow their example today?
- Imagine a version of yourself that's happier, and name them. Sometimes I picture "Neat Ruby" — she picks up after herself. She keeps a refreshing, houseplant-filled room. I motivate myself to clean by thinking of that person I want to become.

Tip #2. Keep a journal—but no pressure!

The main reason I was never able to keep a journal around was because I felt this constant pressure to write in it every day. I didn't wanna sit down and go, "Dear diary, today I heard from Cindy that Tommy likes Jessica…" And so I never did! My nice fancy decorative journals were all abandoned after two or three entries.

The best way to make journaling fun is to make it as low stakes as humanly possible. It's only for you, and it's okay to mess up! Here's what I've been doing for the last few years:

- Get an ordinary composition book. I like the grid paper ones. They're about two dollars at any office supply store. Write "Total Honesty" on the front with a sharpie.
- Set aside a page for an index.
- *Only write when you have something to write about!* Give your entry a fun title at the top like, "Here's why the ending of Neon Genesis Evangelion was bullsh*t," and write one page about that.
- Shorter thoughts and ideas can go in the back of the book.

Tip #3. Pay attention to your body. Everyone has an innate sense of right and wrong. You may have learned to suppress that, because oftentimes it's easier or safer to just do what other people want. Or you may not have learned to read the signals behind your feelings. Every emotion comes from a place in the body. Happiness feels like a tickle running up from my chest to my head. Sadness twists and aches in my throat and behind my ribcage.

If you're doing something and you get a sensation in your stomach that just feels like, "Yuck!" stop and reflect on why that is. If I'm about to make a decision and my insides feel queasy, I make sure to hold off for a moment and ask myself, "Is this wrong for me? Will this hurt me in the long run? Will it hurt someone else?"

Tip #4. Just fake it. If you have absolutely no clue who you're supposed to be— it's okay to try things on. Sip coffee and eavesdrop at your local cafe, gazing wistfully out the window. Wear a bandana and herd goats. You create the person you are a little bit every day. You can change every day too. Put on a thousand costumes. Eventually you'll find your clothes.

CHAPTER 10

Learn to be alone.

Everyone knows the feeling: you finally get through the day, feeling like a used kleenex. Then, the second your head hits the pillow, all the thoughts you didn't have time for during the day hit you in a flood of existential dread. You can see your entire life laid out in front of you like a flower always unfolding. Or maybe it's the past you visit, flashing scenes of a childhood you didn't realize you remembered so well. Your lower back is screaming at you to succumb, but you don't fall asleep for a long time.

I don't think I was consciously aware of it, but when I was depressed, I feared that moment of clarity more than anything else. More than death, even. I would cross the street without looking twice, but I couldn't make myself close my eyes while my brain still had legs to run on. I'd do everything to avoid hearing my loud thoughts echo in an empty head. I knew being alone was dangerous without being able to articulate why.

I was so focused on the thrill of the chase, the sweat on my brow, the pound-thud of my heart, wheezing lungs, aching feet—

I was so caught up in running away, I couldn't look back to see what I was even running from. Think of any good horror movie: in Alien, we don't see a xenomorph until fifty-seven minutes; in Jaws, it takes an hour and twenty-one minutes to show the shark. The not-knowing only made my fear more potent. Here is what I did know: I couldn't remember the last time my mind had felt like a safe place to enter alone. So, I stayed up every night until I passed out— scrolling through twitter, texting, getting fashion tips from Wikihow, and reading comics under the bedsheets. Anything to never discover what was hiding in the darkness behind my eyelids.

A relationship in crisis is not always easy to see. The parties involved might act in a way that appears normal to outsiders. In the same way, it can be hard to notice when you are avoiding yourself. A person's relationship with their own self requires many of the same things as a relationship with another person:

It requires kindness and understanding, definitely. But it also requires quality time. Just like an afternoon bickering over chores does not constitute a mother-daughter bonding day, simply being alone for a few minutes after school or during a test isn't an appropriate substitute for meaningful introspection. It's not "me time." A good relationship with the self— and good mental health in general— relies on having a bit of time to wonder, feel, experience, and think in peace.

The only way to stop viewing my own mind as a hostile environment was to spend some quiet time there alone. And to do that, I'd need to face off against something I was taught had to be unpleasant: boredom.

In order to do that, it turns out, all I had to do was look at it from a different perspective. Really, it's all about input and output. At school, you might be taking in loads of information: people talking, bells ringing, teachers lecturing, and the entire internet blasting you with distractions. Then you might be heaving all that back out, taking tests, yelling at your siblings, talking to customers at work, and answering the impossible question, "How are you?"

That's the *value* of boredom. If you're always either taking in information or giving it out, you might never be bored, but your mind is in *constant flux*.

Where's the time to *generate* thoughts, form opinions, and *experience* your life? Nothing can grow in soil that's always being tilled. So now I know what I was so afraid of when I wouldn't let myself sleep.

I was scared that, once I started having thoughts of my own, I wouldn't be able to go back to the comfortable busy static silence I'd grown used to. I was both right and wrong about that. I was right in that I couldn't go back, not if I wanted to, not if I tried.

But I was also wrong, because letting my mind wander wasn't uncomfortable at all. It started slowly and undramatically, like all good things. I felt it that very first fall, every time I took the long city bus ride over the bridge into Austin for my 8 AM Russian class. I'd pause the music blasting from my headphones and just listen to the sound of my breath, the brakes hissing, that robotic voice repeating safety instructions in Spanish. *Por favor no cruce enfrente de bus.* I'd look at the other people on the bus drifting to sleep and bumping their heads against the windows. I'd learn how to put my phone down and just watch that pale dawnlight shatter over glass skyscrapers and yellow grass.

I'd notice things I hadn't noticed before— How the street lights flickered off one by one down the street like a line of fireflies, or how the last one at the very end glowed pink instead of white. When I got off the bus and started walking, I'd notice the smell of early morning rains on the asphalt. I'd see the shining granite capitol, watch the grackles' frenzied black wings as they fought for balance on a phone line. It was like waking up a leg that had lost circulation; I was overwhelmed at first, but that was the price of regaining sensation.

Death, college, and the phases of the moon came to mind calmer than they ever had before. The less I avoided quiet, the less violent my thoughts became, like the difference between an inhale and a gasp. I suppose they finally had time to space themselves out. I'd finally get to campus with enough time to buy a honey bun from the vending machine and share it with a congregation of sparrows in the courtyard. *Am I lonely?* I'd think.

No, I'm just alone.

STORYTIME: A RAPTURE ON THE LONELY SHORE

When I was fifteen, I never did any thinking at noon or over breakfast so my thoughts would come bite at my ankles in the night. Frantic senseless mutterings rushed in all at once the second I closed my eyes. All day it was Twitter and research and texting Jaz and the beat of the music ever-present in my ears; it was getting hard to hear people in the cafeteria at school. "I'm sorry, could you repeat that?" was the price I paid for music loud enough to block out anything I didn't want to feel, which was anything at all, anything real.

I had an obsession with fiction, see. Anything I could get my hands on was fair game for constant reworking, projection, and analysis. When I read a book, I was transporting my mind to a new world, renting a reality. The problem with the internet is that it's possible to enter a new reality without recognizing that you have left your own. With fanfiction, Tumblr, and roleplaying I found worlds that weren't my own and instead of exploring them briefly as a vacation, I took up permanent residence. Often, I'd spend so long roleplaying on some forum I'd just forget to eat until it was two in the morning and a day's hunger twisted bitter in my gut.

It was the perfect escape—as close as I could get to becoming someone else. Through fictional works and reworks, sharing memes and encoding messages in playlists, I said things and felt things that would've been too risky for the real world of solid consequences and sharp boundaries. I could express all my feelings and fears through these fictions, and it kept them in the safe soft fuzzy zone of the ostensibly fabricated.

The first time that world broke underneath me, it was sunset. This was by design: in those long early summer months after I dropped out, my walks in Elliott Ranch at dusk were the only time I ever came close to quieting the static fuzz of constant stimulation. This time, I skipped the music and walked in silence for a stretch leading up to the gate.

In that bowl-shaped neighborhood, where mist bleached the tops of cedar trees and faded sky into earth, I began to see things in startling clarity. It was a distinct feeling of coming into my body— was I just a brain sitting in a jar before? I stood and walked on shaky legs past ostentatious McMansions with cordial lawn lights. Vibrancy and excitement rattled through everything in the world like a breeze through trembling lilac leaves.

This sharpness won't hurt me. I heard my breath as I mouthed the words to myself. I heard my heartbeat. I saw the pitch winding outline of a live oak's branches reaching skyward, shaking, alive. I smelled the grass all around me, and it didn't smell dirty like you'd expect; it smelled sweet. Street lamps blinked on in a line, one by one like fireflies, and the very last one glowed pink.

I need to stop running away, came my next thought, faster than I could speak. *I need to delete my twitter, burn my phone, go off the grid, run away into the mountains and live in a cave only sustained by superstitious gifts from the quiet fishing town below. Wait, focus. I can't keep ignoring reality because I'm scared. Why am I scared? What am I scared to think? It's beautiful. It's terrifying. I'm here, I'm alive, I hate it— thank God.*

I didn't want to go inside my house after that; it felt too much like an ending. I lingered on the porch, watching bugs hop around our overgrown front garden and planning my escape from every bad habit I'd ever collected and sewn too tightly to my heart.

Eventually, I did step inside; ten minutes of passion was enough for me. The next day I fell into the same patterns I always had, crowding out my mind with other people's thoughts.

It's funny how you can know exactly what's right for you and refuse it— again, again.

Why do we do that?

I didn't want anything to matter—so I became the internet. I knew all, but I focused on nothing. I was instantly gratified. I talked without listening. I shared everything but beheld nothing. I had knowledge of the world without experiencing it. And Vriska fought Lord English, and Harry found the Horcruxes, and Patroclus died for Achilles, again and again, and I laid in bed doing nothing at all, and in my world of fiction, it didn't matter one single bit.

But I kept having moments like that— flashes of clarity to break up the static soft comfort of rushing from thing to thing without ever stopping to think, *am I happy? Is this how I always want to live— when I'm 18, when I'm 30?* I learned to stretch those memories around my shoulders and wear them as armor against self-destruction. I knew what it felt like to be fully *in* the world, so I also knew that I usually wasn't. I came to recognize when I was ignoring my conscience, with what tools, and I constantly questioned which of my hobbies were working for me; once I started truly looking, a lot became apparent.

Drinking didn't make me happy; it only obscured and delayed despair. Posting on Instagram never once made me feel proud of myself. Even after talking on the internet all day long, I was still lonely.

It was more fun to save my good jokes for friends instead of twitter; I could see them laugh right in front of me.

Trying to stay off the internet while carrying a smartphone around is like trying to stay on a diet with a chocolate fountain in your room. It makes no sense.

Though it was full of stops and false-starts, I slowly took action. I deleted my social media accounts, one by one, and found that I felt unburdened rather than deprived.

Now more than ever, I spend a lot of time alone. My friends who were seniors in high school last year, and that's most of them, have all graduated and moved to New York or Portland or anywhere else. And I'm still here. I don't use social media— I quit that last November, and this summer I stuck my T-mobile SIM card into a little black flip phone. I bit the bullet on that one, I really did it. The big *what if* is settled: yes, the flip phone has helped me stay focused. I'm still learning how to text with T-9.

And you know what? I never really had anything to fear at all. I'm not falling apart because I have to spend some days by myself— I'm stronger. All that's changed is, I get to decide who knows me. I get to decide who sees me. When I'm lounging in the soft itchy grass beneath a post oak tree, or eating lunch or sitting on the porch with my potted cacti looking out for shooting stars, anytime I have an interesting thought or notice something funny, it doesn't go on Twitter for the world to see. It's mine. Either I write it in my little grid paper journal, save it in my head for only me to enjoy, or tell it to a friend when I can really hear them laugh.

There's a sense of peace and security I feel know that I am not always connected that I never knew before. A defiance. When my phone is dead, I don't panic. I'm not restless. "If somebody needs me," I say, "They can come find me."

I just breathe deep and watch the world turn, the cause-and-effect chain reaction exploding through every second. Ground-to-grass-to-tree-to-birds-to-sky, everything swaying and churning;

there is motion everywhere in this cosmic Rube-Goldberg machine we call a planet. It's better than imagination.

So maybe living in fiction was good for me; maybe distraction was what I needed when reality seemed too huge and awful to face. I don't regret the past, and all the times I found my willpower too weak. I don't regret the ways I coped badly with my fear. But now— I say this with excitement—

Now I want to live.

> "There is a pleasure in the pathless woods
> There is a rapture on the lonely shore,
> There is society, where none intrudes,
> By the deep sea, and music in its roar:
> I love not man the less, but Nature more"
> — Lord Byron

HOW TO FIND SOME QUIET, MAKE FRIENDS WITH BOREDOM, AND GIVE YOURSELF A BREAK:

Tip #1. Learn how "too much" feels. I have invented a word for the opposite of lonely. This is something I think we, as a society, have made a mistake in forgetting to name.

In times long-past, people were lucky to get a newspaper every day. They owned few books. They did slow activities like playing dominoes and pool— and spent much of their time either working or alone. The word I've invented didn't need to exist, so nobody thought of it.

Now I think so many people feel this way so much of the time, we haven't named it for reasons of constancy rather than absence. At least that's why I hadn't thought of it before. How does a fish know it's in water? I could not name a sensation I was hardly ever free from.

It's a bit silly, but my word is "crowdy." As in,
*When one is **alone** and must seek the society of **others**, one is **lonely**.*
*When one is **crowded** with others and must seek the society of **oneself**,*
*one is **crowdy**.*

See, just as you can feel lonely in a room full of people, you can feel crowdy when there's no one else around. Whatever you choose to call it, just recognizing that this feeling exists is a step in the right direction.

Tip #2. Find time for a bit of solitude throughout the day.
- Pick a household task you usually do while listening to music or the radio. Do it quietly.
- Do you take public transit? Do you drive or carpool? Try taking your trips in quiet, just in your own company for a while. Notice the people, plants, and animals outside.

- Take yourself out on a date— go to a movie or a nice restaurant by yourself some time. When I went to school downtown, I liked to get a turkey and cheese at Thundercloud Subs and eat it on the patio overlooking Shoal creek.
- Watch the sun rise or set— just sit outside and see the world slowly turning.

Tip #3. Consider using the internet less. I don't mean to complain about the technology like a stodgy old person who hates electric light —I like the internet. I just distrust the idea that *always together* is better. I distrust the way so many of us seem to use the internet not to be together, but to avoid ever being alone. There will always be some shocking new tweet, some show, some game, some photo, some video, some moronic op-ed or fad or meme. Is there time for other things? Really consider whether your current use of the *internet* (if you do use the internet) is enjoyable and useful, or if it's simply a distraction.

Tip #4. Take a day off. 24 hours. Don't work, don't study. Unplug your phone. Some religions call it the Sabbath. I think that traditions— whether religious or not— can make a day very special. It all depends on what feelings and activities you find relaxing.

Here are my personal favorite things to do when I can get a day off:

- Lighting candles.
- Warm baths.
- Tending my cactus garden.
- Reading a trashy romance novel.
- Making hibiscus tea.
- Eating fruit all day.
- Lying in the sun.
- Walking at sunset.
- Watching the stars come out.

Afterword

It's not like you go through one phase of life, one set of struggles, and then the Earth stops turning, and you never have problems again. The universe doesn't offer anyone a "happily ever after."

If it did, it certainly wouldn't happen at age seventeen.

So yeah. I still have my problems. I'm mad about politics, I get lonely, I fall into ruts and get into fights. My life isn't "solved." I have days every few months when I wonder, "What am I doing? Is all this worth it?"

'Cause being alive is a wild ride!
I don't know what's in my future.
But I can imagine it, now.
Living a good life.
Getting older.
Falling in love.
Seeing so many sunsets.
Smiling at my reflection in a puddle on the street.
Giving something to the world that I can be proud of.

And to me, that's worth everything.

Acknowledgements

First, I'd like to thank my whole family. They've done everything for me and writing this would've been impossible without their support.

Mom, you encouraged me to work on this book even when I was being a wildly neurotic about it. I guess that's just the producer in you. For all the writing practice I've gotten, words still can't express how much I admire you – your wit, your wisdom, your jokes and your laughter. You've made my life amazing and I love you.

Sean, thanks for everything you taught me about art and taking it easy. For better or for worse, I have your morbid sense of humor now. I'm lucky to be your daughter.

Dad, thanks for the good times, all over the world. I hope the moon's shining on you.

Chance, thank you for being a great friend and an amazing brother. Everything I've done in my life has been with you at my back. Long live the IB of CLJDRW!

Jack, thank you for understanding. I always felt like we could talk when things were bad. You have a huge heart, and you're hilarious. Stay gold.

Uncle David, you were the reason I believed people could change. The dedication you have for everything you do inspires me, and you're funny as heck to boot! Thank you.

Mary Cary, thank you for reading my drafts and helping me grow as a writer. For our conversations, and for your stories. I love you, Meema!

I'd also like to thank my friends. I don't mention them enough in the text of this book, because most of it was happening inside my head, but my friends stuck with me through good times and bad, and I would've been lost without them. Thank you to:

Al, for that letter you wrote me the winter before it all went pear-shaped. And everything since.

Mars, for always dreaming up a future with me.

Talls, for being a genius, but dumb enough to stick around.

Carl, Tosca, and every member of the Political Cultures class of 2016 — you gave me more than you know. Disco was never just a phase.

Maia, Ash, Brough, Tess, Renae, Evan, and Gill — Thanks for being part of this story!

And finally: to Dr. Megha Adlakha and the staff at Family Dentistry on Manchaca—thank you for being so supportive, and for fixing my teeth!